THE SCHOLASTIC ENCYCLOPEDIA OF
SPACE

JACQUELINE MITTON AND SIMON MITTON

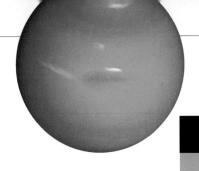

A Marshall Edition
Edited and designed by
Marshall Editions Ltd
The Orangery
161 New Bond Street
London W1Y 9PA

First published in the U.S.A. by Scholastic Inc.
555 Broadway, New York, NY 10012

Library of Congress Cataloging-in-Publication Data available.

10 9 8 7 6 5 4 3 2 1   9/9 0/0 01 02 03 04

ISBN 0-590-59227-0

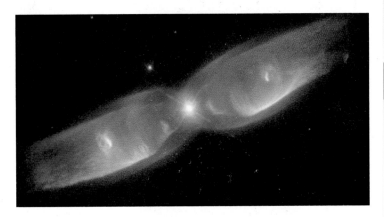

Consultant, United States:
Frank Summers
Hayden Planetarium
American Museum of Natural History
New York, New York

Originated in Italy by Articolor
Printed and bound in Italy by
Officine Grafiche de Agostini

First Scholastic printing,
August 1999

△ **A "Twin Jet" nebula**
The double star at the
center of this nebula is
sending out two high-
speed streams of gas,
like a pair of jet engines.

Top The blue color of the
planet Neptune is due to
the methane gas in its
atmosphere.

Previous page A *Hubble
Space Telescope* image
shows a glowing nebula
in the spiral galaxy, M33.
More than 200 massive
stars lie at the center of
the nebula.

CONTENTS

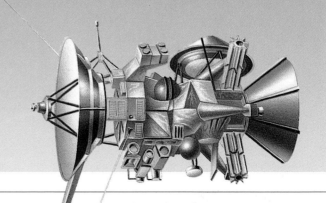

THE UNIVERSE

The universe is huge. It includes Earth and all of space—the Sun, the Moon, other planets, stars, and galaxies. Astronomy is about exploring and understanding our universe.

The photograph *(left)* shows bright stars, glowing gas, and dust in the Milky Way Galaxy.

SEEING INTO SPACE

On a clear, dark night, the sky invites you to the greatest show on Earth. You do not need a telescope to get started. Your eyes are good enough to look billions of miles into space. You will see hundreds of stars in the night sky. You may see the Moon and some planets. Our planet Earth, the Moon, and eight more planets and their moons belong to the Sun's family—the solar system. The solar system and all the stars you can see belong to the Milky Way Galaxy, our home galaxy. Using telescopes, astronomers can see much more. They can see millions of faint stars belonging to our galaxy, and the stars of other galaxies beyond.

▷ **What is out there?**
The nearest objects to Earth are our sun and the planets, moons, and comets of the solar system. The solar system belongs to a galaxy containing billions of stars and great clouds of gas and dust. Our galaxy shows in the night sky as the Milky Way. It is just one of countless galaxies in the universe. The picture shows a map of the whole Milky Way.

The Moon
Earth's nearest neighbor in space is its moon. There is no atmosphere or liquid water on the Moon.

Comets
A comet is a ball of ice and dust orbiting the Sun. As it comes closer to the Sun, it forms a tail of gas and dust.

4

THE KECK TELESCOPES

The two largest optical telescopes in the world are at the Keck Observatories in Hawaii. Each telescope has a huge main mirror measuring 33 feet (10 meters) across, which is kept exactly in place by a computer. The twin telescopes can be linked together. Operating like a giant pair of binoculars, they will see greater detail than any other telescope.

The main mirrors
Each of the two mirrors is made up of 36 six-sided pieces, which fit together like tiles.

Galaxies
Beyond the Milky Way Galaxy, millions of other galaxies populate the universe. Each is a family of billions of stars similar to our own galaxy.

Bright nebulae
Huge clouds of gas are made to glow by the stars buried inside them. There are many of these bright nebulae between and around stars in our galaxy.

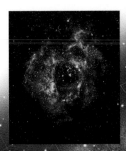

GALILEO GALILEI

Although he did not invent the telescope, Galileo Galilei (1564–1642) was the first person to use one for astronomy and the first to write down what he could see. He made many telescopes in his workshop in Italy. In 1610 Galileo discovered four moons going around Jupiter. He also found that the hazy light of the Milky Way comes from many faint stars. His discoveries immediately made him famous.

Galileo (right) and one of 60 telescopes he designed (below)

Stars
On a clear night you can see hundreds of stars in the sky. The nearest stars are thousands of times farther away than any planet in the solar system.

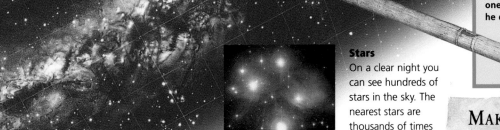

Planets and moons
The nine major planets in the solar system have at least 63 moons among them. Other stars in our galaxy might have planets and moons, too.

PLANETS, STARS, AND GALAXIES

The Sun, the planets, and their moons are the main things in the solar system, but there are asteroids, comets, and lots of dust as well.

The Sun is the nearest star to Earth. The stars of the night sky are all similar to the Sun but, because they are much farther away, we see them only as points of light. Stars are extremely hot balls of glowing gas, which give out large amounts of energy and shine with their own light.

They are generally much larger than planets. Unlike stars, planets and moons do not produce their own light but shine in the sky because they reflect the light of the Sun. The stars are separated by distances much greater than the size of the solar system. The next nearest star after the Sun is nearly 300,000 times farther away.

On a very dark, cloudless night you can sometimes see the light coming from billions of distant stars in our galaxy—we call it the Milky Way. It looks like a hazy arch of light sweeping across the sky. When we see the Milky Way, we are looking toward the center of our galaxy.

MAKING SENSE OF THE SOLAR SYSTEM

EARTH-CENTERED SOLAR SYSTEM

Earth

Moon

Sun

Planets in motion
More than 2,000 years ago, Greek astronomers knew of only five planets in our sky. They thought that the Sun, the Moon, and the planets circled around the Earth. In 1543, Nicholas Copernicus described the solar system with the Sun at the center. Observations Galileo made with his telescopes helped show that Copernicus was right.

COPERNICUS'S SUN-CENTERED SOLAR SYSTEM

Sun

Earth with Moon in orbit around it

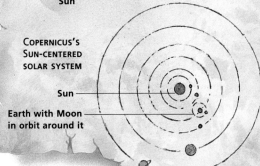

LOOKING BACK IN TIME

Time as distance
The light that made this photograph of a galaxy set out on its journey across space 51 million years ago. We say the galaxy is 51 million light years away.

Distances between stars and galaxies in space are enormous. Astronomers often describe such large distances by giving the time it takes for light to travel that far. In the same way that we might say a journey is a three-hour drive in a car, astronomers might say that the distance of a star is a 100-year journey for light. Because light takes so long to reach us from galaxies beyond our own, we see these galaxies as they were long ago. Looking deep into space with a powerful telescope is the same as looking back in time.

SPEED OF LIGHT

Light travels at just over 186,000 miles (almost 300,000 kilometers) in one second. Nothing can travel faster than light. The Sun is 93 million miles (150 million kilometers) away from us. A spaceship flying from the Earth to the Sun would take about a year, yet light takes just eight minutes to cross the same vast distance. In one year light travels 5,900,000,000,000 miles (9,500,000,000,000 kilometers). We call this distance a light year.

The farther away a star or galaxy is from Earth, the longer its light takes to reach us. The nearest star after the Sun is more than four light years away. This means that it takes four years for light from that star to reach us and we see it as it was four years ago. One of the nearest galaxies to our own is at a distance of 2 million light years. The light we see today from this galaxy started its journey 2 million years ago, before humans like us existed on Earth.

We do not know what this galaxy is like now; we only know what it looked like 2 million years ago.

Large telescopes show us galaxies *billions* of light years away. When we look at these galaxies, we are seeing back in time by billions of years, to when galaxies were first forming. So a telescope is a kind of time machine.

NEPTUNE
Distance from Earth:
4 light hours

4 hours ago

MOON
Distance from Earth: 1.3 light seconds

SUN
Distance from Earth:
8 light minutes

8 minutes ago

EARTH

Looking back
The farther away an object is, the longer its light takes to reach Earth. This means that astronomers can look back in time. For example, light from Neptune takes four hours to reach Earth, so astronomers see Neptune as it looked four hours ago. By comparing galaxies billions of light years away with ones a lot nearer, they can see how galaxies have changed. The most distant galaxies we see today came into existence long before the Sun and its planets formed in our galaxy. They show us what galaxies were like soon after they were created.

Hubble Deep Field

This very special picture includes the faintest galaxies ever seen. It was made by putting together 342 separate observations by the *Hubble Space Telescope (see box at right)*. It is called the Hubble Deep Field. Concentrating on a tiny speck of sky, the *Hubble Space Telescope* discovered 1,500 galaxies. Galaxies 10 billion light years away and only one-tenth the age of our Milky Way Galaxy appear as little smudges. Their light was halfway here before Earth even existed.

HUBBLE SPACE TELESCOPE

Launched in April 1990, the *Hubble Space Telescope* (or *HST*) orbits Earth. Above Earth's turbulent atmosphere, it has a much clearer view of the universe than any telescope on the ground. Astronauts have gone to the telescope in the space shuttle twice—in 1993 and 1997—to put problems right and replace old parts. The *HST* has a main mirror measuring 94 inches (2.4 meters) across. It has taken images of every kind of object from planets to the farthest galaxies we have ever seen. Astronomers hope the telescope will help them discover the size and age of the universe. It was named after the astronomer Edwin Hubble *(see page 11)*.

2 million years ago

4.3 years ago

ANDROMEDA GALAXY (the nearest large galaxy)
Distance from Earth: about 2 million light years

antenna

PROXIMA CENTAURI (our nearest star after the Sun) Distance from Earth: 4.3 light years

light coming in from space

In orbit around Earth

The *Hubble Space Telescope* circles Earth every 90 minutes in an orbit 380 miles (610 km) above us. The telescope's power comes from two solar panels—one on either side—which turn sunlight into electricity. Astronomers on the ground control the telescope and collect its observations by means of radio signals.

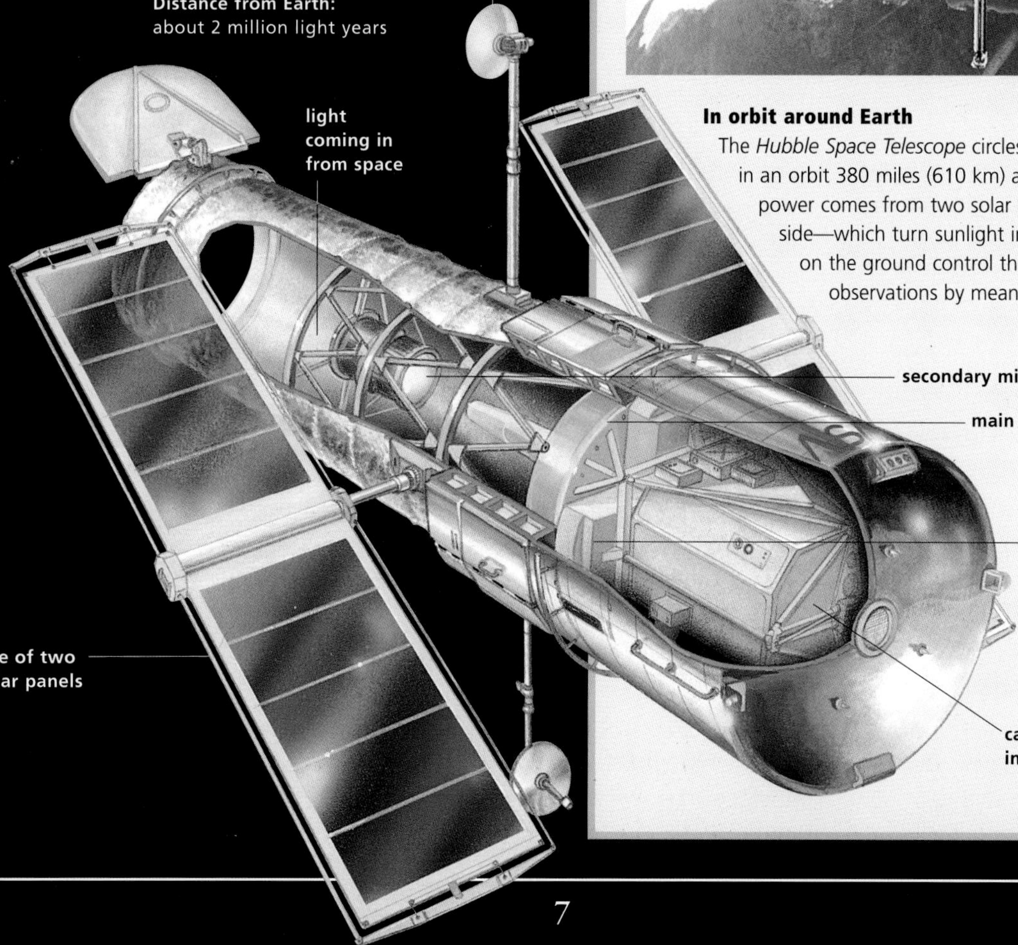

secondary mirror

main mirror

sensors for guiding telescope

one of two solar panels

cameras and instruments

THE BIG BANG

Our universe began about 15 billion years ago in a massive explosion known as the Big Bang. The universe emerged from an incredibly tiny and extremely hot burst of energy. At first it was nothing like the universe today. It consisted almost entirely of energy. But in the first millionth of a second, most of the energy turned into matter. Every substance that exists—solid, liquid, or gas—is made of matter. The whole universe, with its matter and energy, expanded rapidly and cooled down at the same time. It has been getting larger and cooler ever since.

THE FORMATION OF THE UNIVERSE

What happened?

The universe came into being in the Big Bang. At first it was very small and very hot, but it expanded fast. As the universe grew, it cooled. Energy turned into matter. After a time, most of the matter was in the form of the gases hydrogen and helium. Gas clouds collected into clumps, pulled together by gravity. The first stars in the universe formed in the clumps, and the clumps merged to make galaxies. Some galaxies collapsed down to form disks in which spiral arms developed.

protogalaxies form, containing the first stars

gas clouds cool

EVENT

the universe just after the Big Bang

the universe expands rapidly and the gases hydrogen and helium form

TIME

one hour after the Big Bang

1 million years after the Big Bang

1 billion years after the Big Bang

AFTER THE BIG BANG

As the universe expanded after the mighty explosion of the Big Bang, and all the matter rushed headlong in every direction, gravity started to play a part.

Gravity rules the universe. It is a force that pulls every object toward every other object. All material has the pulling power we call gravity. The most massive things—those with most material in them—pull strongest.

The force of gravity makes all matter want to collect together.

So when the universe was only a million years old, matter in the form of the gases hydrogen and helium was already beginning to draw together and settle into slowly spinning clumps called protogalaxies. These would make the very beginnings of galaxies. Small clumps of gas inside the protogalaxies became stars.

Protogalaxies were like huge star clusters or dwarf galaxies. They mostly formed in groups and were the building blocks for galaxies. Drawn together by gravity, protogalaxies began to collide and merge. At first, they made small galaxies with odd shapes. Eventually, enough protogalaxies merged to create the larger spiral and elliptical galaxies we see today.

But that is not the end of the story. In many galaxies, new stars kept forming. Galaxies are still merging and changing. Even today, new stars are being born in the Milky Way Galaxy, and a dwarf galaxy is in the process of merging with it.

Voids and walls

Over time, galaxies started to gather in clusters and sheets separated by vast empty regions called voids. Voids are like bubbles in a foam, with galaxies and clusters of galaxies forming the walls around the bubbles.

protogalaxies start to merge to form galaxies

large galaxies form—some become spirals

3 billion years after the Big Bang

5 billion years after the Big Bang

COBE AND COSMIC RIPPLES

The *Cosmic Background Explorer (COBE)* satellite was launched in 1989. Its main job was to detect the warmth left over from the Big Bang, which is called the cosmic background radiation. *COBE* made a map of the temperature of the whole sky and found small differences, rather like ripples. In the map, the blue regions are cooler than average by a tiny amount, and the red regions are warmer. The background radiation *COBE* measured dates back to half a million years after the Big Bang. The tiny variations over the sky show that the universe had stopped being the same throughout by the time it was only half a million years old. Once the universe had stopped being smooth and uniform, matter began to gather into clumps.

The *COBE* satellite *(above)* mapped the background radiation in the universe *(left)*.

GALAXIES IN SPACE

A galaxy is a family of billions of stars that are held together in space by the pull of gravity. Galaxies are not spread evenly throughout the universe. They are mostly arranged in great sheets, strings, and groups. Some are in large families called clusters. Galaxy clusters can have thousands of members all held together by gravity. Many clusters of galaxies are grouped into even bigger families, called superclusters. A typical supercluster contains about 12 galaxy clusters and is hundreds of millions of light years across.

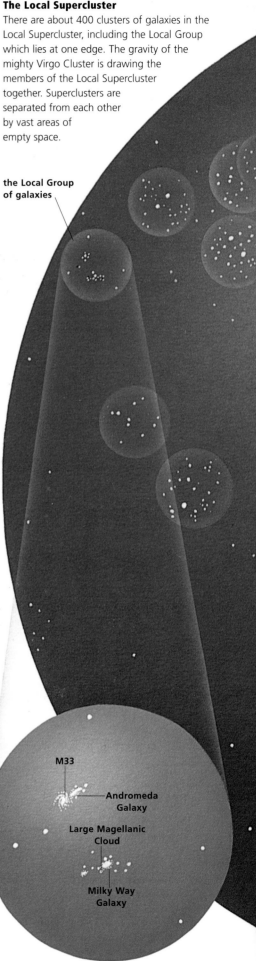

The Local Supercluster
There are about 400 clusters of galaxies in the Local Supercluster, including the Local Group which lies at one edge. The gravity of the mighty Virgo Cluster is drawing the members of the Local Supercluster together. Superclusters are separated from each other by vast areas of empty space.

the Local Group of galaxies

M33

Andromeda Galaxy

Large Magellanic Cloud

Milky Way Galaxy

The Virgo Cluster
This photograph shows part of the Virgo Cluster, which is a family of several thousand galaxies 50 million light years away. The two brightest galaxies in the picture are M86 *(near the center)* and M84 *(at right)*. The most massive galaxy in the Virgo Cluster, M87, is pictured on page 13. Its immense gravity helps to hold the cluster together.

OUR NEIGHBORHOOD

The Milky Way—our home galaxy—belongs to a cluster of about 30 galaxies scattered across 3 million light years. Known as the Local Group, it is a very small cluster of galaxies—many galaxies are in clusters with hundreds or even thousands of members. Nearly all the members of the Local Group are small (or dwarf) galaxies. Many are very dim and have only recently been discovered. The Local Group lies close to the edge of a family of about 400 clusters of galaxies that belong to a supercluster, which we call the Local Supercluster.

MOVING GALAXIES

Measuring how far galaxies are from us tells us about the layout of the universe today. But to predict the layout of the universe in the future, we need to know how galaxies are moving.

Collecting information on the distances and speeds of many clusters of galaxies reveals that the more distant a cluster of galaxies is, the faster it is

racing away from the Milky Way. One reason why astronomers know the universe began with a Big Bang is the way galaxies are rushing apart as if from a massive explosion. However, it is not that the galaxies are moving *through* space. Instead, space itself is stretching as the universe expands from its tiny beginnings.

The pull of gravity between all the galaxies is slowing the expansion of the universe. For a long time, astronomers have wondered whether gravity will eventually stop the expansion and pull all the galaxies back together again so the universe ends in a "big crunch." But after peering far into the universe with the most powerful telescopes, astronomers now think it likely that the universe will expand forever.

The Local Group
Of the 30 or so galaxies that make up the Local Group, there are only three large members: the Milky Way Galaxy, the Andromeda Galaxy, and a spiral galaxy called M33. There are nine dwarf galaxies close to the Milky Way and a further eight near Andromeda.

EDWIN HUBBLE

One of the greatest astronomers of the twentieth century, Edwin Hubble (1889–1953) identified individual stars in the nearby galaxy M33 and showed that it is a family of stars beyond our Milky Way Galaxy. Having proved that there are galaxies beyond our own, he went on to show that these galaxies are moving away.

When a galaxy is moving toward or away from us, the light we receive from it looks a different color from when it is still. A galaxy moving away appears redder. It is said to have a redshift.

A galaxy coming nearer looks bluer. It has a blueshift. This change in color is called the Doppler effect.

Using the Doppler effect, Hubble measured the speeds of galaxies and made the astonishing discovery that the farther away a galaxy is, the faster it is moving. He found that the speed of a galaxy is directly linked to its distance. Today the relationship between the speed of a galaxy and its distance is called Hubble's Law. It shows that the whole universe is getting bigger.

Edwin Hubble (left) showed that M33 (above) is a galaxy beyond our own

the Virgo Cluster

The Large Magellanic Cloud, our neighbor
This medium-sized galaxy belongs to the Local Group and is a satellite galaxy of the Milky Way. This means that it orbits the Milky Way Galaxy. The Large Magellanic Cloud takes more than 2 billion years to make one circuit and is 165,000 light years away. It has 20 billion stars.

A GALLERY OF GALAXIES

Galaxies come in many varieties, with different sizes, shapes, and masses. Some are naturally faint. Others pour out immense amounts of light and heat. All galaxies are families of stars. Many also contain clouds of gas and dust. The tiniest galaxies have just a few million stars and are only a thousand light years in size. The largest galaxies have millions of millions of stars and are hundreds of thousands of light years across. Just three galaxies are visible to the naked eye from Earth, as faint, misty patches of light. But there are billions and billions visible with large telescopes. Many thousands of galaxies lie in a patch of sky the size of the full moon.

Spiral galaxy NGC 2997
This galaxy is similar to the Milky Way Galaxy. Two spiral arms emerging from the center contain young stars, glowing clouds of gas, and some streaks of dust.

SHAPES OF GALAXIES

Most galaxies are elliptical, shaped rather like a football. Giant ellipticals have ten times as many stars as the Milky Way Galaxy, but they are quite rare. Most ellipticals are dwarfs made up of just a few million stars.

Spiral galaxies are bigger and brighter than dwarf elliptical galaxies. They contain between a billion and a trillion stars and usually have two main spiral arms curling out of a bulging center. The arms may be anything from tightly wound to loose and open. As a spiral galaxy turns slowly around its center, its arms seem to trail along. The appearance of a spiral galaxy depends on our angle of view, because it is a flattish

Barred spiral galaxy NGC 1365
In about one third of spirals, the arms wind out from the ends of a central bar of stars rather than directly from the core (or nucleus).

object. From above, we can see the spiral pattern of the arms. From the side, we see the central bulge and often a dark streak due to a layer of dust.

More than a third of all galaxies do not have a regular shape. These are called irregular galaxies. They are usually smaller than spiral galaxies and contain a lot of gas. Some galaxies are irregular because they have been distorted by the pull of gravity of another galaxy nearby.

Dwarf elliptical galaxy Leo 1
Less than 1,000 light years across, and only 750,000 light years from Earth, this is one of the ten nearest galaxies.

CLASSIFYING GALAXIES

A simple code is used to describe the basic shape of a galaxy. "E" means an elliptical galaxy. "S" means a spiral. An elliptical is also given a number according to how flattened it looks. For example, "E0" is like a sphere, "E2" is lemon shaped, and "E7" is like a short but fat cigar. The codes for spiral galaxies are "Sa" for tightly wound arms, and "Sb" and "Sc" for more open arms. The arms of some spirals seem to wind from the end of a bar at the center of the galaxy. Their code is "SB."

elliptical galaxies			spiral galaxies			spirals with bar		
E0	E2	E7	Sa	Sb	Sc	SBa	SBb	SBc

COLLIDING GALAXIES

In the crowded regions of large galaxy clusters, individual galaxies may get close enough to collide with each other. It takes millions of years for one galaxy to crash right through another. The pull of gravity of each galaxy distorts the disks and spiral arms, and can cause long spindly streamers of stars to fly off into deep space. It is unlikely that any stars bang together head-on because stars are tiny compared to the wide spaces that separate them. Gas clouds crashing into each other do get squeezed, and this may cause new stars to form rapidly.

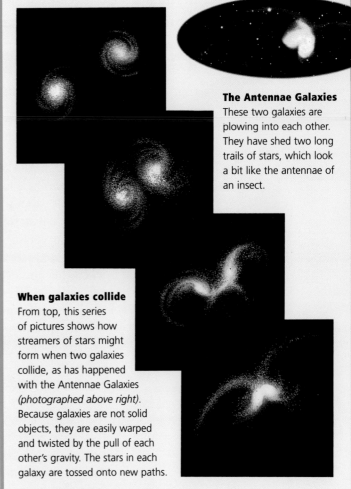

The Antennae Galaxies
These two galaxies are plowing into each other. They have shed two long trails of stars, which look a bit like the antennae of an insect.

Spiral galaxy M65
This is a sideways look at a normal spiral galaxy. Dense clouds of dust packed into the spiral arms can be seen as a dark line stretching across the disk.

When galaxies collide
From top, this series of pictures shows how streamers of stars might form when two galaxies collide, as has happened with the Antennae Galaxies *(photographed above right)*. Because galaxies are not solid objects, they are easily warped and twisted by the pull of each other's gravity. The stars in each galaxy are tossed onto new paths.

Elliptical galaxy M87
This giant elliptical galaxy of type E0 has the same mass as 10 billion billion Suns.

The Cartwheel Galaxy
The small galaxy on the right crashed through the ring-shaped galaxy on the left. The shock of the encounter set off a burst of star formation all around it. We see the new stars as a ring of light.

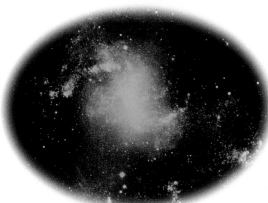

Irregular galaxy NGC 1313
A recent burst of star births has broken up the normal spiral pattern in this galaxy.

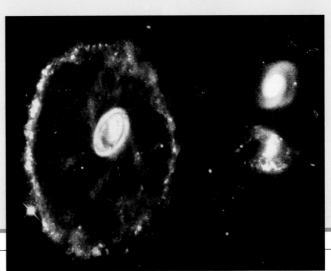

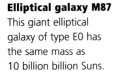

ACTIVE GALAXIES

Light from normal galaxies comes to us mostly from their stars. However, some galaxies have a different way of making light, which can make them dazzlingly bright. Known as active galaxies, they produce incredible amounts of energy from their centers, where they are probably being powered by huge black holes.

Quasars are the centers of the brightest active galaxies. They are the most energetic objects in the universe. Because galaxies with quasars in them are hundreds of times brighter than ordinary galaxies, they can be detected at much greater distances.

Radio galaxies channel much of their extra energy into huge clouds that give out strong radio waves.

Cygnus A
Two giant clouds of matter, one on either side of the Cygnus A galaxy, send out radio waves. The clouds stretch across one million light years of space. Cygnus A produces a million times as much radio energy as the Milky Way Galaxy.

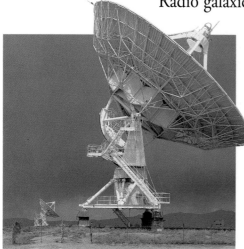

Radio telescopes
This is one dish of the Very Large Array—a set of 27 radio telescopes on a site in New Mexico. Each dish is 80 feet (25 m) in diameter, but linked together, they gather as much information as a dish several miles or kilometers across. Using linked radio telescopes, astronomers can probe inside active galaxies.

RADIO GALAXIES

Astronomers first found active galaxies about 50 years ago, when they had started looking for different types of energy coming from objects in space. They got a big shock when they discovered that some far-off galaxies give off powerful radio waves, sending out far more energy as radio waves than as visible light. Active galaxies of this kind are known as radio galaxies.

A typical radio galaxy has two giant clouds of matter that lie far outside the main galaxy. The clouds look as if they have been blasted out to either side of the galaxy. Most of the radio waves come from these clouds, not from the galaxy itself.

QUASARS

Thirty years ago, astronomers discovered quasars. Many quasars, though not all of them, give off radio waves. However, it is the visible light from a quasar that is most important. In a telescope, a quasar looks like a brilliant star, but it is actually the core of a galaxy at least 100 times brighter than a normal galaxy. The galaxy around the quasar is usually too faint to be seen. All of the extra light is pouring out of the quasar at its center.

Images of quasars and radio galaxies sometimes show two bright, narrow jets of light and energy shooting out from either side of the central region.

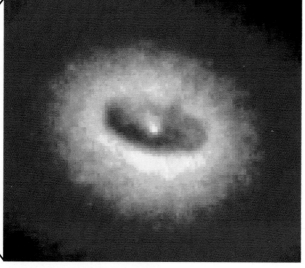

Radio galaxy NGC 4261
The long, colored blobs on either side of galaxy NGC 4261 *(far left)* show where jets from the center of the galaxy are giving out huge amounts of energy as radio waves. Very near the center *(left)*, a dark disk of gas 300 light years across is swirling around a bright core. This close-up, taken by the *Hubble Space Telescope*, provides strong evidence that a black hole millions of times more massive than the Sun is lurking there.

THE POWER AT THE CENTER

Active galaxies, such as radio galaxies and galaxies containing quasars, produce far more energy than their stars can make. Apart from the jets, there is other evidence that something dramatic is going on. In many active galaxies we can see matter swirling around the central region at colossal speeds. In a few cases we can also detect a pancake shape of hot gas spinning at the center. This makes astronomers think that active galaxies probably contain gigantic black holes. Located at the center of a galaxy, a black hole sucks in matter of all kinds, including stars and gas. As the matter plunges toward the black hole, some of it is sent spinning around in a disk. Some matter bounces back before reaching the black hole, making the bright jets above and below the disk.

The central black hole pulls material toward itself by gravity. As stars and gas plunge headlong toward this black hole, enormous amounts of energy are given off. In the most powerful galaxies, the black hole has grown to a few billion times the mass of the Sun.

jet

central region

energy given off

spinning disk of matter

black hole

A typical active galaxy
The total size of an active galaxy like this one may be 100,000 light years or more across. However, most of its energy is generated in a central region of just a few hundred light years or less where a rotating disk of hot gas is falling into a black hole (see inset picture).

Jets blasting into space
Some of the gas swirling around the black hole in the middle of an active galaxy is squirted out to form a pair of high-speed jets. These jets create the great radio clouds detected to either side of radio galaxies and some quasars. They can reach for hundreds of thousands of light years

WHAT IS A BLACK HOLE?

A black hole is a region of space with such high gravity that nothing escapes its grip, not even light. When you jump up, it is the Earth's gravity that pulls you back down to the ground. To escape the Earth's gravity, you would need to jump at a speed of 7 miles (11 kilometers) per second. Because the Sun's gravity is 30 times more powerful than Earth's, its escape speed is 384 miles (618 kilometers) per second. The stronger gravity pulls, the harder it is for you to escape from it. A black hole is a region of space where gravity pulls so hard that even light traveling at 186,000 miles (300,000 kilometers) per second cannot escape. No light comes out, so a black hole looks black.

light easily leaves the surface of the Sun because it travels much faster than the speed needed to escape the Sun's gravity

Sun

event horizon

black hole

any light inside a region around a black hole called its event horizon cannot escape at all—the escape speed there is greater than the speed of light

THE MILKY WAY GALAXY

Our home in the universe is the Milky Way Galaxy, a family of 100 billion stars mixed with great clouds of gas and dust. If we could look at our galaxy from far out in space, we would see it is a spiral similar to many of the galaxies we can see beyond our own. The galaxy formed about 14 billion years ago from a giant, slowly turning ball of gas. The force of gravity pulled the gas inward so that the ball gradually collapsed to form a thin disk with a bulge in the middle. In the very center of the galaxy there is a black hole.

A SPIRAL GALAXY

We cannot see to the center of our galaxy because dust gets in the way. But radio waves travel easily through dust, so radio astronomers have been able to map the Milky Way Galaxy. They show that it is like any other giant spiral galaxy, with a central bulge and curving arms where there are gas clouds and young stars. Some stars lie in a huge sphere around the galaxy. This sphere is called the halo. The stars in the halo have been there since before the galaxy collapsed down to a disk.

From a central region less than 10 light years across, radio waves and heat energy are pouring out with the strength of 80 million Suns. Amazingly, the main source of energy is a zone no larger than the orbit of Jupiter around the Sun. A black hole millions of times more massive than our Sun lies at the center, sucking in matter and making energy.

There is more to the Milky Way Galaxy than we can see. Its stars move as if they are attracted by something. There seems to be a huge amount of invisible material surrounding the galaxy. No one really knows what the dark matter is, but some astronomers guess that it is dead stars.

Interstellar material
Clouds of dust and gas between the stars, called interstellar material, form the Horsehead Nebula and its surroundings. The dark horse's head shape is mainly tiny particles similar to soot and sand, and it is part of a much larger dark cloud. The red and blue light behind the dark silhouette comes from glowing gases

From the outside
The Milky Way Galaxy is shaped like a thin pancake with a big bulge in the middle. Spiral arms, made of gas, dust, and young stars, emerge from the central bulge. The galaxy contains billions of stars, which are packed much closer together in the bulge than in the arms. The Sun lies a little more than halfway from the center to the edge of the disk. The galaxy rotates, and the Sun takes 220 million years to make one circuit.

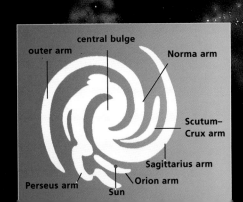

- outer arm
- central bulge
- Norma arm
- Scutum–Crux arm
- Sagittarius arm
- Perseus arm
- Orion arm
- Sun

▷ A galaxy profile
This side-on view of the Milky Way Galaxy shows the central bulge and the disk with a layer of dust running through it. In a ball-shaped halo around the whole galaxy there are about 200 globular star clusters. These clusters were the first stars to form in the galaxy and are very old. Their positions show that the galaxy was once shaped like a sphere.

THE MILKY WAY GALAXY IN CROSS-SECTION

globular cluster

halo

bulging center of galaxy

layer of dust

disk

A globular cluster
Omega Centauri is a globular (or ball-shaped) cluster of stars 600 light years across. It contains hundreds of thousands of the oldest stars in the galaxy.

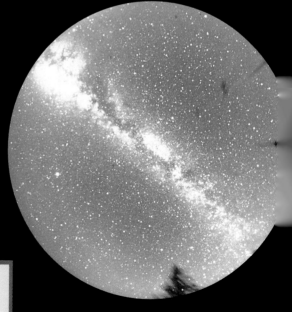

MILKY WAY FACT FILE

Size of Milky Way Galaxy:
100,000 light years across

Distance from Sun to center of galaxy:
28,000 light years

Thickness of disk:
1,000 light years

Central bulge: 10,000 light years thick; 15,000 light years across

Number of stars:
100 billion

Time taken for Sun to orbit around center of galaxy:
220 million years

The center of our galaxy in the night sky
Looking toward the center of the Milky Way Galaxy, which is in the direction of the constellation Sagittarius, we see a much greater concentration of stars than anywhere else in the sky. The dark areas with fewer stars are clouds of dark dust, which cut out the light of the stars beyond.

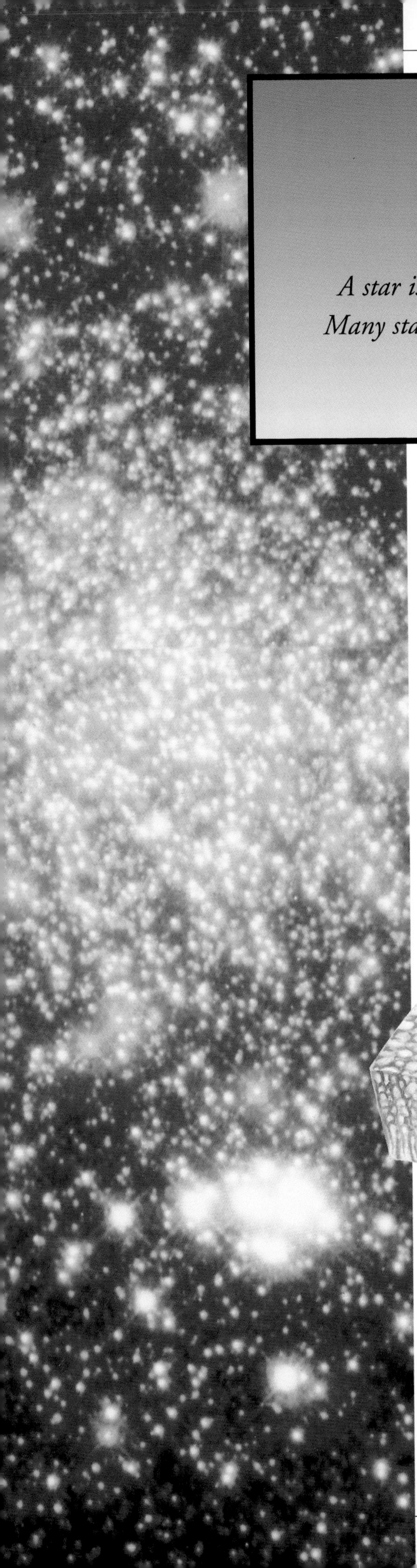

THE STARS

A star is a huge ball of hot gas, heated from inside by nuclear energy. Many stars are similar to the Sun, but there are also giants as big as the entire solar system and dwarfs as small as Earth.

The photograph *(left)* shows two star clusters, each containing thousands of stars.

THE SUN

The Sun is the solar system's star. It gives Earth the heat and light that are essential for life on the planet. Because the Sun is only 93 million miles (150 million kilometers) away, astronomers can find out far more about it than about any other star. We know that it is like a bubbling cauldron, with vast quantities of energy seeping out into space at the surface. We know that it has a strong magnetic field that causes some dramatic effects, such as flares and sunspots. Careful study of the Sun is important for working out how its changes can affect Earth, so special telescopes and space observatories are used to monitor the Sun.

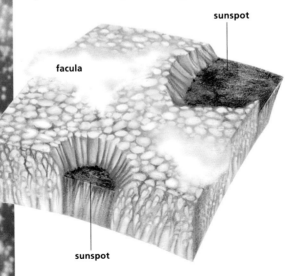

sunspot

facula

sunspot

▽ Prominences
Tongues or arches of hot gas called prominences are often seen over the Sun's surface. Some last for many weeks. Others surge up violently and last only a few hours. They can leap tens of thousands of miles into space.

prominence

△ Spots on the Sun
Sunspots are dark looking areas where the Sun's magnetism is especially strong at its surface and cools it down. A sunspot can cover an area much larger than Earth. Individual sunspots last no longer than a few weeks, but the overall number varies enormously over a cycle lasting 11 years. Sometimes an extra bright area, called a facula, can be seen nearby. The temperature of a facula is higher than that of its surroundings.

HEAT AND LIGHT

The Sun's surface is called the photosphere, and its temperature is about 10,000°F (5,500°C). Above the surface there is a hotter layer of atmosphere called the chromosphere, with a temperature of 27,000°F (15,000°C). The outermost layers of the Sun's atmosphere are called the corona. The corona extends for millions of miles, and its temperature near the Sun is 2 million°F (1 million°C). Gases from the corona stream off into space as the solar wind, which blows with a speed of 500 miles (800 kilometers) per hour.

Like all stars, the Sun generates nuclear energy. Deep inside, the temperature is a searing 27 million°F (15 million°C). At this temperature, the particles of gas that make up the Sun react together to turn hydrogen into helium and energy. As the energy is released, the Sun loses mass. In fact, every second the Sun gets 4 million tons lighter! But it is not going to disappear any time soon. It has been 5 billion years since the Sun was formed, and it is still only halfway through its supplies of hydrogen fuel.

Many changes on the Sun are linked to its magnetic field. Being made of gas, the Sun rotates faster at its equator than at its poles. The magnetic field in the gas stretches and winds itself around the Sun, rather like an elastic band. When it cannot stretch any farther, the magnetism breaks up and releases energy, which we see as solar activity.

SOHO SPACECRAFT

The *Solar and Heliospheric Observatory (SOHO)* was launched in late 1995 with 12 instruments on board. It orbits the Sun 930,000 miles (1.5 million kilometers) nearer the Sun than Earth, at a special point where its distance from Earth does not change much. *SOHO* was designed to study the solar wind and the Sun's atmosphere. It can also detect movements in the Sun's surface layers, which help astronomers to work out what the inside of the Sun is like.

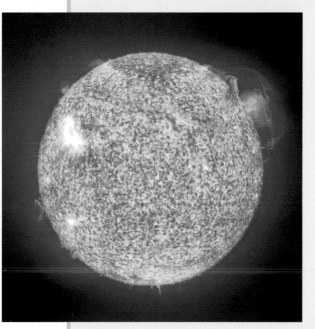

◁ **The Sun from *SOHO***
This is an ultraviolet light picture of the Sun, taken by a special camera on *SOHO* (pictured right).

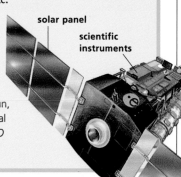

solar panel

scientific instruments

▽ **An active surface**
Solar flares are explosions on the Sun's surface, which blast particles into space. They can cover an area larger than the Earth. Smaller spikelike spicules last a few minutes and are a few thousand miles high. The bubbling of the Sun's surface gives it a varying mottled pattern, called granulation.

flare

CORONA

CHROMOSPHERE

PHOTOSPHERE

Earth (to scale)

spicule

◁ **Lights in the sky**
Material blown out from the Sun breezes past Earth and causes changes in Earth's upper atmosphere, mainly near the poles. Gases in the atmosphere glow as a result. We call the display the aurora, or the northern or southern lights.

sunspot

SUN FACT FILE

Mass (the amount of matter it contains): 333,000 times Earth's mass

Radius: 433,000 miles (696,000 km); 109 times Earth's radius

Surface temperature: 10,000°F (5,500°C)

Central temperature: 27 million°F (15 million°C)

Composition: 70% hydrogen, 28% helium, 2% mixture of other materials

Age: 5 billion years

WARNING: The Sun is extremely bright. You should never look straight at it, even with sunglasses, or you may seriously damage your eyesight. Take care when using binoculars or a telescope that you don't accidentally point them toward the Sun.

The Pleiades
The stars in this bright cluster are only 50 million years old. The dinosaurs were already extinct on Earth when they first blazed out in the sky. Often called the Seven Sisters, the Pleiades can easily be seen by the naked eye in the constellation Taurus.

STAR BIRTH

The oldest stars in our galaxy were born about 14 billion years ago. New stars have been forming ever since. Stars are born in vast, dark clouds of cold gas and dust. The force of gravity pulls clumps of gas together to make the beginnings of a star. At first the forming stars are hidden from our view behind cloaks of dust. We know the young stars are there only from the invisible infrared light they give out, which is detected by special telescopes. But once the stars are fully formed, they break through the darkness and light up the remaining gas around them in a blaze of color. The Orion Nebula is the nearest cloud where we can see all this happening.

STAR BIRTH IN THE ORION NEBULA

Orion in the sky
The constellation Orion, the Hunter, is one of the brightest and most familiar patterns in the sky (1). Below the three stars that form Orion's belt lies a misty patch of light that is visible in a dark sky even without a telescope. This glowing cloud of gas is called the Orion Nebula (2).

1

2

THE ORION CLOUD
The Orion Nebula is a small part of something much bigger: the huge, dark Orion cloud. If this cloud were visible in the sky, we would see that it extends across most of the constellation Orion. But the only way astronomers can tell it is there is from the invisible forms of energy it sends out, such as infrared light and microwaves. The Orion cloud is about 1,300 light years away and 100 light years across.

A wave of star formation has been working its way through the Orion cloud for the last 12 million years, leaving star clusters in its wake. When new stars are established and are shining strongly, their activity clears the gas and dust out of

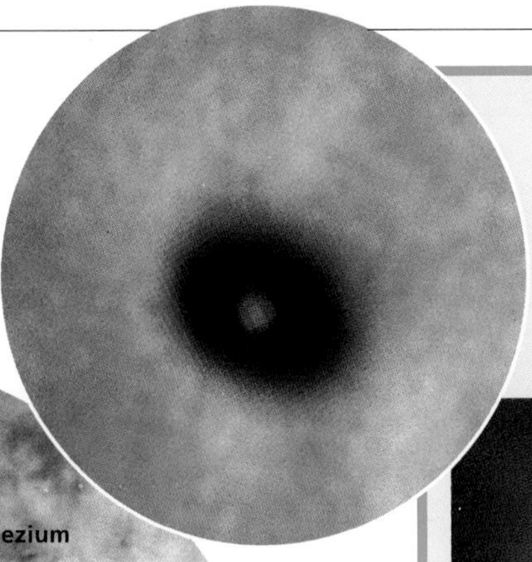

Trapezium

4

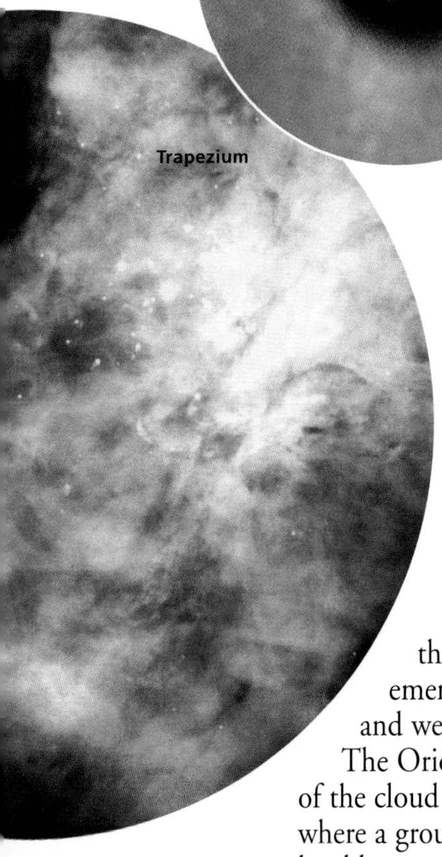

STELLAR NURSERIES

Stars form in clusters rather than on their own. A cluster might contain anything from a handful to hundreds of stars. When we see a cluster of stars in the sky, we know they all formed together. After stars have formed, their presence can set off a new wave of star birth nearby. Over time, the stars in a cluster gradually drift apart. All the stars now scattered through our galaxy were once in clusters.

1. A cluster of brilliant young stars has just emerged from the dark cloud of gas and dust from which they formed.

2. Hot gas from the young stars triggers the formation of more stars just inside the nearby cloud.

3. The first cluster spreads out. The second cluster emerges and sets off the formation of yet another cluster.

3

Inside the Orion Nebula

The Orion Nebula glows because of four very hot young stars, called the Trapezium, which lie inside it (3). They are only 100,000 years old. Nearby, more stars are being born.

The Hubble Space Telescope has revealed disk-shaped clouds of gas and dust around some of these newly forming stars (4). Astronomers suspect that families of planets will form from the material in these disks.

their neighborhood. They emerge from the dusty shrouds, and we can see their visible light.

The Orion Nebula—the only part of the cloud we can see—is a place where a group of very hot, young stars has blown a bubble in the dark cloud. These stars are giving out strong ultraviolet light, which makes the inside of the bubble glow. Because the bubble was near the edge of the cloud, it broke through and burst open. Now we can see the stars inside and the bright inner surface of the bubble.

There are many other clouds in our galaxy where stars are being created, but the Orion cloud is the largest known.

THE MAKING OF A STAR

The first stage of star formation happens when gravity pulls clumps of gas together. As the gas particles collect into a ball, they are crammed closer and closer together, which makes them heat up. The ball gets hotter and hotter in the middle. Eventually the temperature inside climbs so high—to several million degrees—that nuclear reactions start to happen and the star is born. This can occur only if the star contains enough material to begin with. With

anything less than one twentieth the Sun's mass, the gas clump gets warm but not hot enough to start nuclear reactions. It glows feebly, then cools off. Stars that fail to light up because they are too small are called brown dwarfs.

When a star forms, a disk of gas and dust collects around it. Material in this disk may collect together to form planets or brown dwarfs. Eventually, a powerful wind of gas blowing off the star clears away any remaining material.

The Eagle Nebula

Clumps of gas with newly forming stars inside them are breaking off these columns of cold gas and dust. This is part of the Eagle Nebula, another cloud in our galaxy where stars are born. The picture shows an area about one light year across.

GIANT AND DWARF STARS

Stars vary in size and brightness. Smaller stars are called dwarfs. Larger stars are described as giants, and the biggest of all are supergiants. The Sun is twenty times larger than a white dwarf star, but supergiants are hundreds of times the size of the Sun. A thousand white dwarfs shining together give out only as much light as the Sun, but there are supergiants as bright as a million Suns.

Stars have different colors, too. Our Sun is an example of a yellow star, but on a clear night it is not difficult to find bright stars that look orange or pure white. In fact stars range in color from blue to red.

BLUE GIANT

Radius: 10 Suns	
True brightness: 800,000 Suns	
Surface temperature: 80,000°F (45,000°C)	

THE SUN

Radius: 1 Sun	
True brightness: 1 Sun	
Surface temperature: 10,000°F (5,500°C)	

CATEGORIZING STARS

We classify stars according to their color and their size.

A star's color tells us its temperature. When a piece of metal is heated, it first glows dull red then changes to bright orange. If its temperature keeps going up, it turns yellow and eventually becomes bluish-white. The same thing works with the gas at the surface of a star, so we can tell what temperature it is. Red stars are the coolest, and bluish stars are the hottest. The temperature of our yellow Sun is in between.

The size of a star is also important. Our Sun is an ordinary star and is small compared with stars tens or hundreds of times bigger. But there are some strange stars that are truly mini-dwarfs if put alongside the Sun. Sometimes balls of gas in space are so small that they never become proper stars at all *(see page 21)*. Astronomers call these brown dwarfs. White dwarfs are old, dying stars that have used up all their fuel. In a white dwarf, as much material as there is in the Sun has been squashed into a ball about the size of Earth.

Stars larger than the Sun
The larger a star, the greater its true brightness. This is the brightness with which it shines in space, rather than the brightness it appears to have when we see it from far away on Earth. A giant or supergiant star gives out more light than the Sun because the area of its shining surface is so much greater than the Sun's. Many of the brightest stars in the night sky are giants or supergiants.

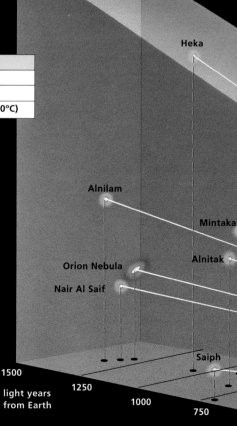

WHITE DWARF

Radius: 0.02 of the Sun	
True brightness: 0.005 of the Sun	
Surface temperature: 45,000°F (25,000°C)	

BROWN DWARF

Radius: 0.1 of the Sun	
True brightness: 0.00001 of the Sun	
Surface temperature: 1,300°F (720°C)	

RED DWARF

Radius: 1/2 of the Sun	
True brightness: 0.05 of the Sun	
Surface temperature: 6,000°F (3,300°C)	

Sun

Stars smaller than the Sun
The Sun is larger than most of the stars in our galaxy. All stars smaller than the Sun give out less light than the Sun. Space is mainly populated by red dwarf stars, but they shine so dimly that very few are visible to the naked eye.

Heka

Alnilam

Mintaka

Alnitak

Orion Nebula

Nair Al Saif

Saiph

1500

light years from Earth

1250

1000

750

RED SUPERGIANT
Radius: 500 Suns
True brightness: 40,000 Suns
Surface temperature: 6,100°F (3,400°C)

Giant Stars

Some stars are born giants. If enough material to make 50 or 100 Suns clumps together as a single star, it turns into a giant 10 or 15 times larger than the Sun. This kind of giant is a very young, very hot star called a blue giant. The temperature in its surface layers can be as high as 93,000°F (52,000°C), and it shines blue-white.

Red giant stars, and even more enormous supergiants, are old stars. They used to be much smaller and have swelled up as their hydrogen fuel has run low *(see page 28)*. Red giants are far cooler than blue ones because their energy is now spread over a much larger area. Their surface layers are only 5,400–7,200°F (3,000–4,000°C).

Star Distances

Two things affect how bright a star looks. One is its true brightness—the brightness with which it shines in space. The other is its distance. Imagine moving any star twice as far away. Of course, it will look a lot dimmer than when it is closer. Now imagine increasing its true brightness. To make it look as bright as it did when it was twice as close, it would have to be four times brighter. Because of this, it is impossible to tell at first sight whether a star is a dim dwarf nearby or a truly brilliant supergiant far away.

To find out the true brightness of a star, astronomers need to know its distance. They can measure this by tracking the small movements a star makes against other stars in the sky. By studying the light from a star astronomers can also find out whether they are looking at a dwarf or a giant.

Stars near and far

Some stars are much more distant than others. The stars making up most of the familiar constellations in the night sky are not necessarily near to each other in space. They just happen to lie roughly in the same direction from our point of view on Earth. The diagram below shows the very different distances of the stars that make up the constellation we know as Orion.

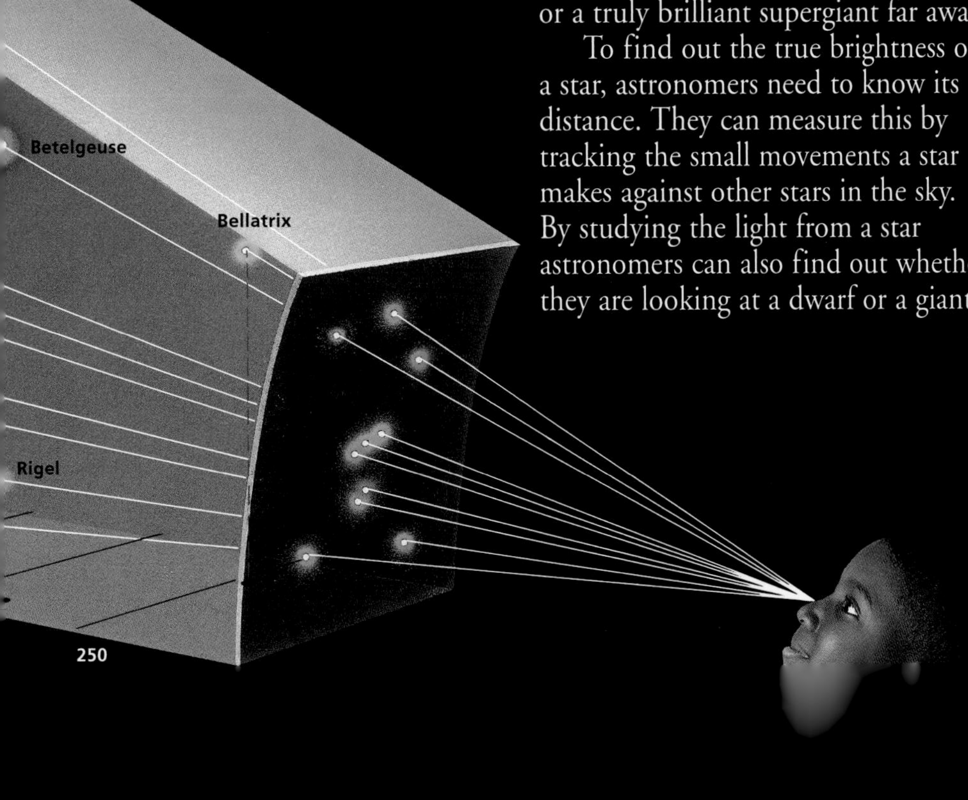
Betelgeuse
Bellatrix
Rigel

Stars with Planets

Detecting planets around other stars is very difficult. But it is possible to tell whether a star is being affected by planets. The gravity of a circling planet tugs on its star, causing the star to move back and forth slightly. This "wobble" shows up in the star's light. By studying the exact kind of wobble, astronomers can tell the mass of the planet and the size and shape of its orbit.

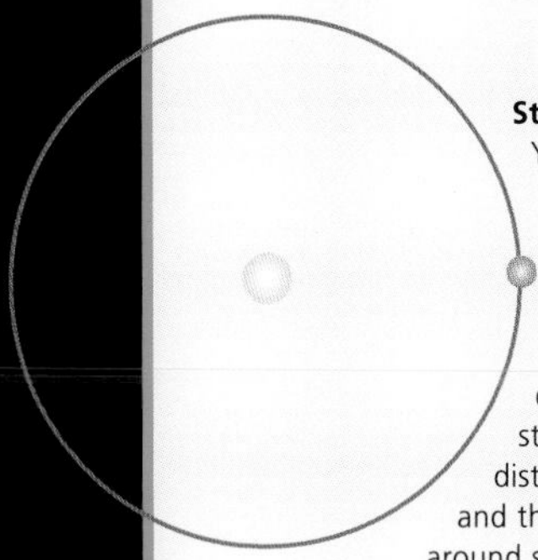

Star: 47 Ursae Majoris Yellow like the Sun; diameter, 1.1 times the Sun's. **Planet:** Probable diameter, same as Jupiter's; orbit, circular; distance of planet from star, 2.1 times average distance between Earth and the Sun; time to go around star (period), 3 years.

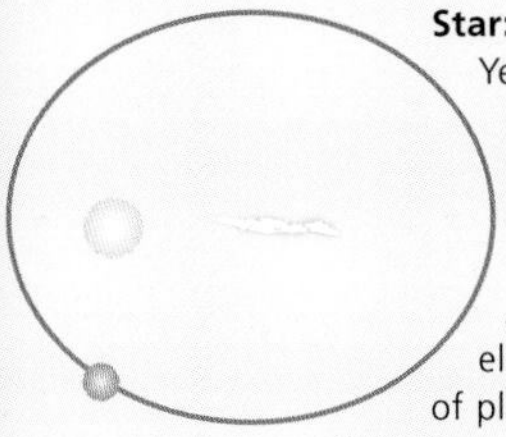

Star: 16 Cygni B Yellow like the Sun; diameter, same as the Sun's. **Planet:** Probable diameter, same as Jupiter's; orbit, very elliptical; distance of planet from star, 0.6 times average distance between Earth and the Sun (closest), 2.7 (farthest); period, 2.2 years.

Scale of distance

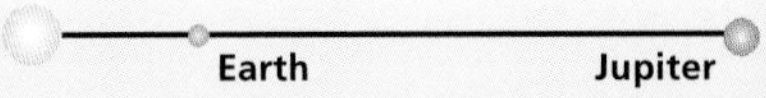
Sun
Earth
Jupiter

Star Fact File

Nearest star: Proxima Centauri, red dwarf, distance 4.25 light years.

Brightest star in sky: Sirius, white star, radius 1.7 Suns, distance 8.7 light years, true brightness 25 Suns.

Star of very high true brightness: Eta Carinae, thought to have the brightness of about 4 million Suns but is hidden behind a dust cloud. It is also one of the most massive known stars at about 100–150 times the mass of the Sun. Distance 8,000 light years.

A very cool, dim star: Gliese 105C, temperature thought to be 4,200°F (2,300°C), true brightness 0.0001 of the Sun.

Hottest known stars: temperatures of about 450,000°F (250,000°C).

VARIABLE STARS

Many stars get brighter then dimmer over and over again. These changing stars are called variables. The variation of some stars is as regular as clockwork. They may take a few days or many months to go through one cycle of brightening and dimming, but the pattern repeats itself exactly time after time. At the other end of the scale, some variable stars spring surprises by flaring up or fading out dramatically without warning. In between, there are stars that follow a general pattern of change but are not always predictable. There are a number of reasons why stars do not keep a steady brightness. That is why variables can behave in so many different ways.

CEPHEIDS

Variable stars of one very important kind are called Cepheids. They take their name from the star Delta Cephei. Delta Cephei takes 5 days and 9 hours to complete its cycle of change. Going from minimum to maximum, it doubles in brightness. The period over which a Cepheid varies can be anything from one to about 50 days. All Cepheids are giant yellow stars several thousand times more brilliant than the Sun. A Cepheid varies because the whole star pulses in and out like a heart beating. Delta Cephei's size swings between 32 and 35 times the size of the Sun.

Cepheids are important because they help astronomers measure distances to galaxies beyond our own. To work out a galaxy's distance, astronomers need to compare how bright its stars seem from Earth with their true brightness. Cepheids are good for doing this because the number of days it takes a Cepheid to vary is always linked to its true brightness.

About 700 Cepheids have been discovered in our galaxy. Astronomers working with the *Hubble Space Telescope* are looking for Cepheids in other galaxies. With the help of Cepheids, astronomers can measure some galaxy distances very accurately. They can then go on to find the size of the universe.

Eta Carinae
Between 1835 and 1845, the star Eta Carinae flared up and became the second brightest star in the sky after Sirius. Now it is barely visible without a telescope. This *Hubble Space Telescope* picture shows clouds of material that came off the star when it flared up. The star is now hidden behind gas and dust.

SOOTY SUPERGIANTS

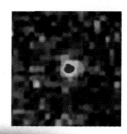

1. A red supergiant star shines at normal brightness.

◁ **A Cepheid variable**
These two pictures taken by the *Hubble Space Telescope* show how the brightness of a Cepheid variable changed over 22 days. This particular star doubles in brightness then fades back to start the cycle again over a period of 51 days.

star begins to expand

star at its hottest and brightest

star at maximum size begins to cool

star shrinks and is at its coolest

star at minimum size

Pulsating stars
Some stars vary because the whole star expands then shrinks again with a regular cycle. The star's color and temperature change as well as its size. They are called pulsating variables. This is how Cepheids vary their brightness. Variable red giants, such as Mira *(see page 25)*, also pulse in and out like this.

HENRIETTA LEAVITT

Working at Harvard College Observatory in Massachusetts, Henrietta Leavitt (1868–1921) made an important discovery about Cepheid variables. In 1895 she began comparing sky photographs taken at different times to find out which of the stars were varying. She discovered Cepheids in a galaxy near to our own called the Small Magellanic Cloud. After studying 25 of them, Henrietta became the first person to realize there is a link between the period of time over which a Cepheid varies and its true brightness.

Henrietta Leavitt

The Small Magellanic Cloud
Henrietta Leavitt discovered Cepheid variables in this neighboring galaxy of the Milky Way. It is visible without a telescope as a small misty patch.

◁ **A smoky star**
In the outer layers of some red supergiant stars, tiny dark particles form, rather like the soot you get from a candle flame. When a lot of soot has collected, it makes the star look very much dimmer. But then the dark material blows off the surface of the star and it returns to its normal brightness. The variations of stars like this are very irregular.

2. The star dims when dark particles like soot form in its outer layers.

3. The star blows away the dark material and returns to normal.

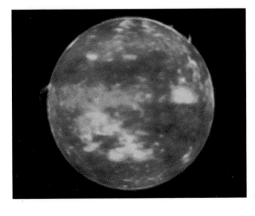

A flare star
In just a few minutes, a violent outburst on the surface of a flare star makes a dramatic increase in brightness. Flare stars are all red dwarfs and the flares are linked to the stars' magnetism.

"WONDERFUL STARS"

One of the most famous of all variable stars is Mira, which can be seen in the constellation Cetus, the Whale or Sea Monster. Mira was the first variable star ever discovered.

In 1596, before there were telescopes, a Dutch astronomer noticed that Mira was a bright star visible to the naked eye. A few months later it seemed to have disappeared, although it did come back eventually. It is not surprising it was given the name Mira Stella, which means

"wonderful star." Now all stars that behave in a similar way are called Mira variables.

Mira is a red giant star that pulses in and out like a Cepheid. But it takes about 332 days to go through a cycle—much longer than a Cepheid—and it does not behave in a very regular way. Mira's visible light fades by a huge amount when the star expands and cools down a little. But all the time the star is giving out most of its energy as infrared rays, which are invisible to human eyes.

DOUBLE STARS

About half of all the "stars" in the sky are in fact double stars. Double stars orbit around each other, held together by the pull of each other's gravity. When two stars are very close, strange things sometimes happen. Material can stream from one star to another, making a bridge between them. If one star swells up into a giant, it can completely swallow the other one. When two stars interact closely with each other, there are often violent consequences—such as powerful bursts of X rays or a nova explosion.

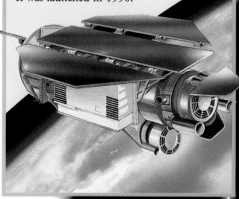

X RAYS

Extremely hot stars and gas in space give out X rays. X rays are powerful and very dangerous to life, but they do not reach Earth's surface, because our atmosphere absorbs them. To study X rays arriving from space, astronomers have to use instruments on satellites in orbit around Earth above the atmosphere. The orbiting X-ray observatory pictured here is the *Roentgen Satellite (ROSAT)*. It was launched in 1990.

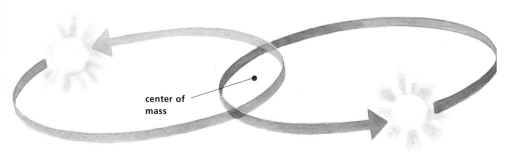

center of mass

Double orbits

Neither star in a double is at the center of the other's orbit. Both swing around a point in space called the center of mass, which is the balancing point between them. Imagine the two stars at each end of a seesaw. The center of mass is where the seesaw would balance.

DISCOVERING BINARY STARS

When a pair of stars are far apart, both may be visible in a telescope. These pairs are called visual binaries. (*Binary* is another word for *double*.) Close pairs can be discovered only by carefully studying their combined light—although we see just one "star" in the sky, its light reveals that it comes from two bodies.

The closer two stars are, the shorter the time it takes them to complete their orbits. Pairs far enough apart to be visual binaries often take tens or hundreds of years. Very close pairs can whiz around each other in a few days—or even a few hours. Because the mass

of a star affects the size of its orbit, astronomers can take the data about the orbits of binary stars and calculate how massive each of the stars is.

ECLIPSING STARS

Because of the angle of some binary stars in space, we can see them cross in front of each other as they orbit. This causes their total brightness to vary. The most famous eclipsing binary is Algol in the constellation Perseus.

ECLIPSING BINARY STARS

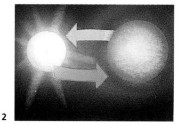

1 2 3 4

Algol
The two stars of Algol circle each other every 2.87 days, crossing alternately in front of each other.

The brighter star is blue-white and the dimmer one is yellow.
1 The blue star is hidden and the total brightness dips strongly over

a few hours. **2** The blue star comes out from behind the yellow star, and the light of both stars is seen.
3 The blue star moves in front of

the yellow star, reducing the total light by a tiny amount. **4** The blue star moves from in front, and both stars show all their light again.

A massive X-ray binary
In this extraordinary pair, a huge blue giant star is held in a binary system with a black hole. The immense gravity of the black hole pulls in streams of material from its partner. Enormous amounts of energy are given off in the form of X rays.

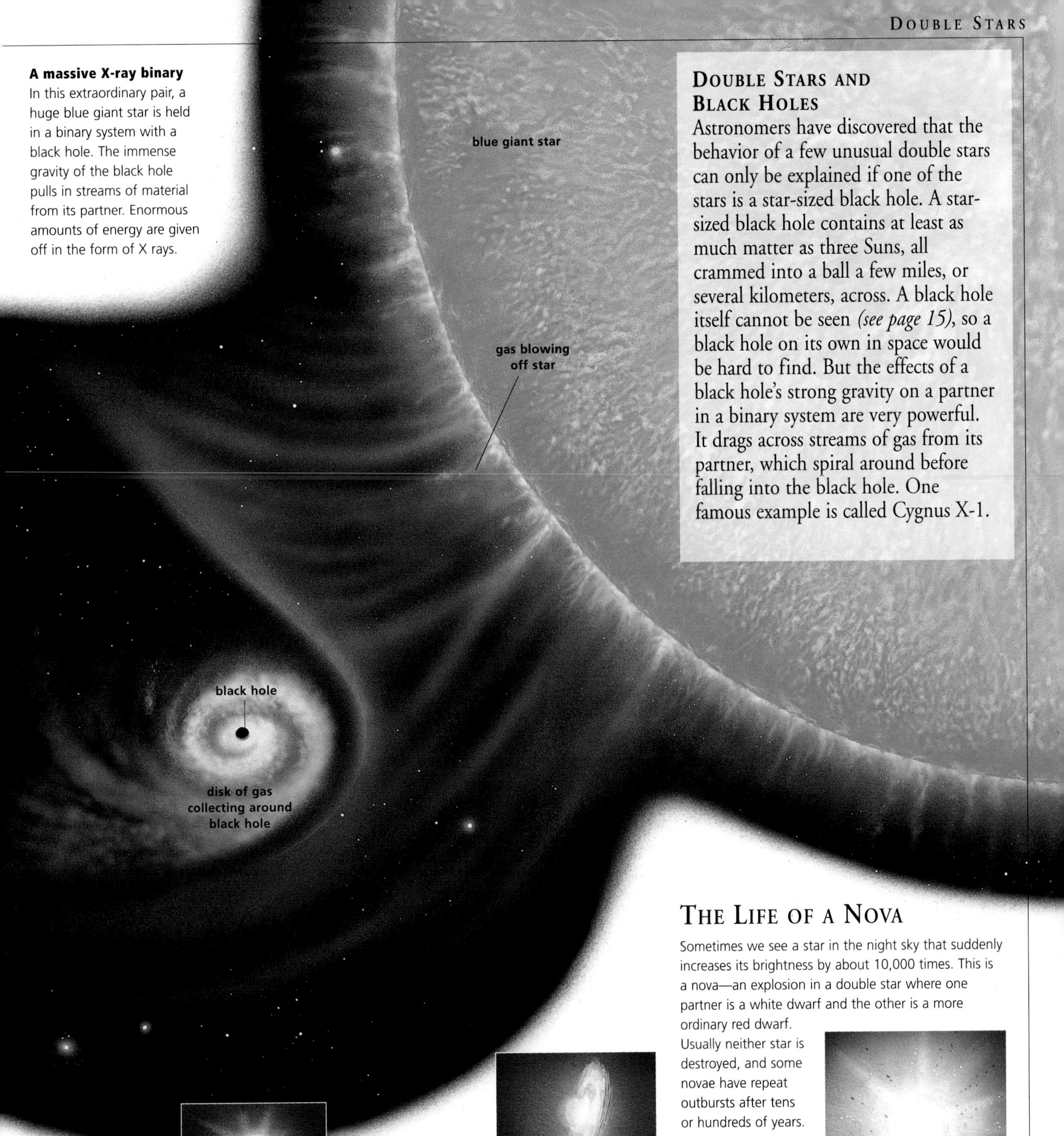

blue giant star

gas blowing off star

black hole

disk of gas collecting around black hole

DOUBLE STARS AND BLACK HOLES

Astronomers have discovered that the behavior of a few unusual double stars can only be explained if one of the stars is a star-sized black hole. A star-sized black hole contains at least as much matter as three Suns, all crammed into a ball a few miles, or several kilometers, across. A black hole itself cannot be seen *(see page 15)*, so a black hole on its own in space would be hard to find. But the effects of a black hole's strong gravity on a partner in a binary system are very powerful. It drags across streams of gas from its partner, which spiral around before falling into the black hole. One famous example is called Cygnus X-1.

THE LIFE OF A NOVA

Sometimes we see a star in the night sky that suddenly increases its brightness by about 10,000 times. This is a nova—an explosion in a double star where one partner is a white dwarf and the other is a more ordinary red dwarf. Usually neither star is destroyed, and some novae have repeat outbursts after tens or hundreds of years.

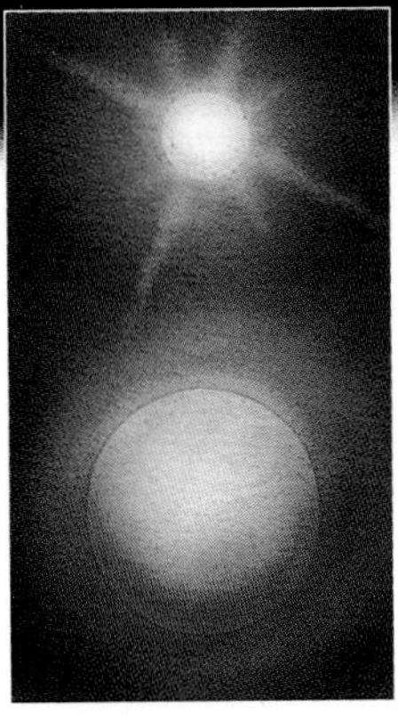

1. This pair of stars will eventually make a nova explosion. The red star is being overheated by the powerful energy from its white dwarf companion.

2. The red star distorts into a pear shape as the strong gravity of the white dwarf draws a stream of gas from it. The gas swirls into a disk then down onto the white dwarf's surface.

3. The white dwarf cannot take the pressure of all the new material. It gets hotter and hotter until a huge and massively bright nuclear explosion takes place on its surface.

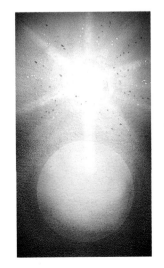

27

DYING STARS

No star keeps shining forever. There comes a time in a star's life when its source of power starts to run out. When this happens, its central core gradually collapses inward, increasing in temperature as it does so. Some of the heat energy released causes the rest of the star to expand outward, and it becomes a giant or supergiant.

Stars of less than about eight times the Sun's mass gradually shed all their outer layers into space. Their cores are revealed as white dwarfs. Stars of higher mass puff off some material, but eventually blow up in a massive explosion, called a supernova. A supernova blasts a great cloud of debris into space, leaving behind either a neutron star or a black hole.

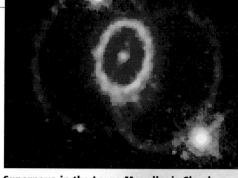

Supernova in the Large Magellanic Cloud
The *Hubble Space Telescope* revealed shells of gas that had been blown off before this star exploded. The debris from the explosion can be seen at the very center.

JOCELYN BELL BURNELL

While studying astronomy at Cambridge University in 1967, Jocelyn Bell Burnell (born in 1943) discovered the beeping radio stars now known as pulsars. One of her jobs was to look through great lengths of graph paper on which signals from a radio telescope were recorded. She realized that some of the strange squiggles must come from unknown objects in the sky. They turned out to be the weird objects called pulsars, which are neutron stars that flash rapid, regular pulses of radio waves toward us as they spin.

Now you see it, now you don't
The regular bursts of radio waves from a pulsar are recorded on paper *(below)*. A few pulsars seem to flash their visible light on and off, too. One that does this is the central star of the Crab Nebula, which flashes 30 times a second *(right)*.

light visible

light not visible

DEATH OF A STAR WITH THE MASS OF 1 SUN

DEATH OF A STAR WITH THE MASS OF 10 SUNS

ordinary star similar to the Sun

large blue star with 10 times the Sun's mass

blue supergiant

RECYCLING IN SPACE
The basic building blocks of everything in the universe are substances we call chemical elements—oxygen, carbon, iron, gold, and many more. Hydrogen and helium were made before the universe was a few minutes old, but all the other elements are made from hydrogen either inside stars or in supernova explosions. When a star dies, the new elements it has made mix into the clouds of gas already in space. So new stars forming in these clouds contain a richer mixture of elements. Our planet is mostly made of elements created in long-dead stars!

ASHES OF DEAD STARS
When stars are finished, all that remains are the cores that used to be their powerhouses. These cores are unlike any familiar material. They have collapsed so much that just a teaspoon of them would weigh many tons! White dwarfs, neutron

△ **Stars of lower mass**
The lifetime of a star depends on how much mass it contains. Lower mass stars use up their fuel at a slower rate and so last longer. Stars like the Sun keep shining without much change for 10 billion years. Then they swell up into red giants. At present the Sun is about 5 billion years old.

△ **Stars of higher mass**
Massive stars use up their energy reserves at a stupendous rate. A star with ten times the mass of the Sun lasts only about 30 million years. It is a large blue star to start with, but it expands and changes color as it gets older.

cloud of gas and dust from which stars are born *(see pages 20–21)*

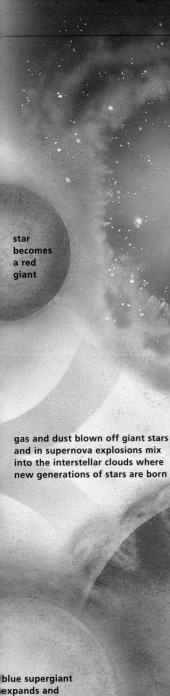

star becomes a red giant

white dwarf gradually cools, becoming dimmer and redder

red giant blows off shells of gas— the collapsed core of the star is revealed at the center as a white dwarf

gas and dust blown off giant stars and in supernova explosions mix into the interstellar clouds where new generations of stars are born

star becomes a red supergiant

blue supergiant expands and gets redder as it gets older

a supernova explosion— the outer layers of the star are blasted off

collapsed core becomes a neutron star or a black hole

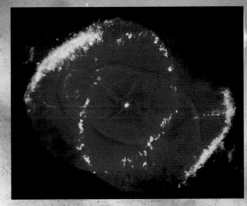

The Cats Eye Nebula
About 1,000 years ago, a dying star blew off its outer gas layers and created this complex pattern of shells and jets. The colors in this photograph were added to show the light from different gases.

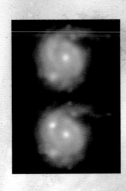

An exploding star
When a supernova exploded in the galaxy NGC 3310, it shone as bright as a billion Suns. You can see the supernova to the upper left of the center of the galaxy in the bottom picture.

stars, and black holes are all different kinds of collapsed star cores. White dwarfs gradually cool down and become dimmer. We cannot detect most neutron stars, but from some we receive short bursts of radio waves. We call those stars pulsars. They spin very rapidly, but gradually slow down. The cores of the most massive supernovae collapse totally into black holes.

The Crab Nebula
Chinese astronomers recorded the explosion of a supernova in the constellation Taurus in the year 1054. Today we see the remains of that supernova as the Crab Nebula, with a pulsar at its center.

THE SOLAR SYSTEM

Nine planets and their moons orbit the Sun, including our own planet Earth. Thousands of rocky asteroids and icy comets also belong to the Sun's family, which we call the solar system.

The photograph *(left)* shows part of the highest volcano in the solar system, Olympus Mons on Mars, from above.

THE SUN'S FAMILY

Seven of the nine major planets in the solar system have more than 60 moons among them. Along with the major planets, several thousand miniature planets circle the Sun. Many are in orbits between Mars and Jupiter. They are called asteroids or minor planets. Comets, which are made of ice and rock, come from the outer solar system.

The Sun with everything in orbit around it, including even tiny particles of dust between the planets, is called the solar system. The Sun keeps its family members in order by the powerful attraction of its gravity. Under the Sun's influence, the orbits they follow are ellipses, which are shapes like squashed circles, although most of the planets' orbits are almost circular.

HOW THE SOLAR SYSTEM FORMED

From gas and dust
1 The Sun, the planets, and everything in the solar system formed 4.6 billion years ago from the same slowly rotating cloud of gas and dust in space. Drawn together by gravity, material collected in a disk around the young Sun.
2 Small clumps came together in the disk. Some collided hard and smashed apart again. Others gently merged to make larger clumps, which were bombarded by the debris that was left.
3 Over millions of years, these larger clumps became the planets we know today. Many smaller chunks of material became comets and asteroids.

SOLAR SYSTEM FACT FILE

| Planet | Distance from Sun (times Earth's average distance*) | | | Time taken for one orbit |
	average	farthest	nearest	(Earth days/years)
Mercury	0.387	0.467	0.308	87.97 days
Venus	0.723	0.728	0.718	224.70 days
Earth	1.0	1.017	0.983	365.26 days
Mars	1.524	1.666	1.381	686.98 days
Jupiter	5.203	5.455	4.951	11.86 years
Saturn	9.539	10.069	9.008	29.46 years
Uranus	19.18	20.09	18.28	84.01 years
Neptune	30.06	30.32	29.80	164.8 years
Pluto	39.5	49.28	29.65	247.7 years

* Earth's average distance from the Sun is 92.96 million miles (149.60 million km).

Jupiter

Mars

Earth

Venus

Mercury

Saturn

THE PLANETS IN ORBIT
The Sun's gravity is pulling everything in the solar system toward it, but planets do not fall into the Sun because of their constant movement in orbit. Their speed balances the pull of the Sun's gravity.

Even as the solar system was first forming, everything was circling in the huge, turning disk of gas and dust that surrounded the newborn Sun. Planets

△ **The planets and their moons to scale**
We call the five planets farthest from the Sun the outer planets. The four rocky inner planets and Pluto are very much smaller than Jupiter, Saturn, Uranus, and Neptune. These giants have large families of moons.

travel slower the farther they are from the Sun. Pluto, the farthest planet, is ten times slower on average than Mercury, the nearest. Pluto also has a lot farther to go on its circuit because it is a hundred times farther from the Sun than Mercury. So Pluto takes more than a thousand times longer to make an orbit than Mercury does.

Uranus

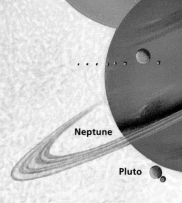

Neptune

Pluto

Pluto

THE ORBITS TO SCALE

Neptune

Uranus

Saturn

Jupiter

orbits of
Mercury, Venus,
Earth, and Mars
(from center out)

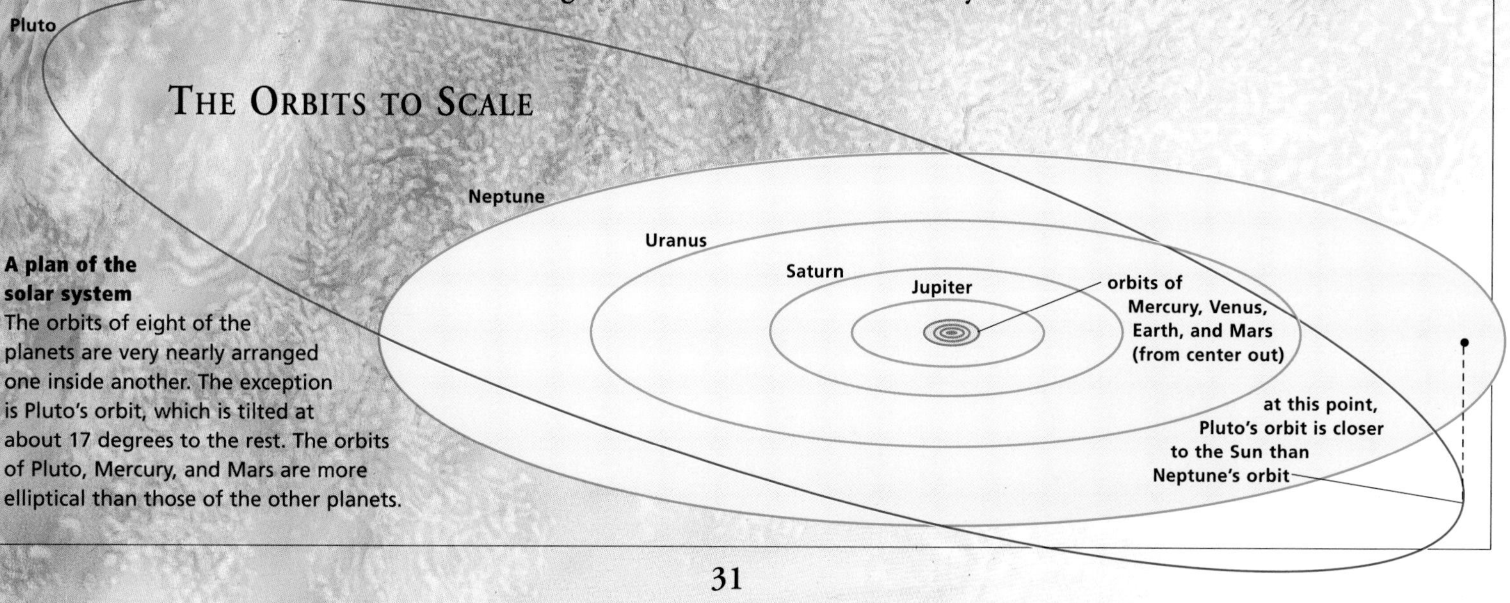

A plan of the solar system
The orbits of eight of the planets are very nearly arranged one inside another. The exception is Pluto's orbit, which is tilted at about 17 degrees to the rest. The orbits of Pluto, Mercury, and Mars are more elliptical than those of the other planets.

at this point,
Pluto's orbit is closer
to the Sun than
Neptune's orbit

31

THE ROCKY PLANETS

The four planets nearest the Sun, together with Earth's moon, are similar in many ways. They are mainly made of iron and rock, and have cratered surfaces. When the planets first formed, about 4.6 billion years ago, there were many left-over chunks of ice and rock circling the Sun. For the next half billion years the inner planets kept crashing into this debris until they had swept up most of it. At first the new planets were very hot, mainly because of all the impacts. Inside they were hot enough for the rock and metal to be molten (or melted). Although the cores of Mercury, Mars, and the Moon have now cooled and hardened, the cores of Venus and Earth are still liquid.

Which planets are rocky?
The inner planets Mercury, Venus, Earth, and Mars (all shown in red), as well as Earth's moon, are made mainly of rock and have solid surfaces.

COMPARING THE ROCKY PLANETS AND EARTH'S MOON

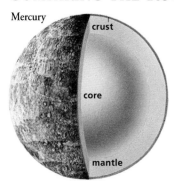

Mercury
- crust
- core
- mantle

Mercury has no real atmosphere, but there is a very tiny amount of gas (mainly sodium and helium) around it.

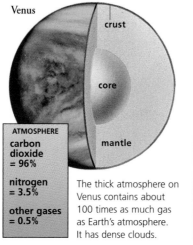

Venus
- crust
- core
- mantle

ATMOSPHERE
carbon dioxide = 96%
nitrogen = 3.5%
other gases = 0.5%

The thick atmosphere on Venus contains about 100 times as much gas as Earth's atmosphere. It has dense clouds.

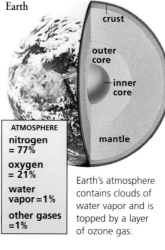

Earth
- crust
- outer core
- inner core
- mantle

ATMOSPHERE
nitrogen = 77%
oxygen = 21%
water vapor = 1%
other gases = 1%

Earth's atmosphere contains clouds of water vapor and is topped by a layer of ozone gas.

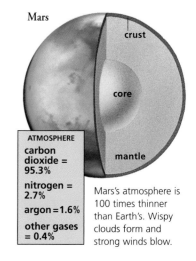

Mars
- crust
- core
- mantle

ATMOSPHERE
carbon dioxide = 95.3%
nitrogen = 2.7%
argon = 1.6%
other gases = 0.4%

Mars's atmosphere is 100 times thinner than Earth's. Wispy clouds form and strong winds blow.

SHAPED BY VOLCANOES

Each rocky planet, and the Moon, has a heavy core of rock or iron. A layer of lighter rock, called the mantle, surrounds the core. On the outside, the solid crust is made of strong rock a few miles thick.

At some time, all the inner planets and the Moon have had volcanic activity, causing deep cracks to open in the crust and hot molten rock called lava to flood out from the mantle

beneath. The Moon, Mercury, and Mars have cooled down and become solid, so their volcanoes are now dead. But lava, ash, and gas still belch out of volcanoes on Earth and Venus. Volcanic eruptions over billions of years let gas trapped inside a planet escape to the surface. This is how the atmospheres of Earth, Venus, and Mars first formed. However, over the last 3.5 billion years, Earth's atmosphere has changed greatly because of plant and animal life.

Giant volcanoes
Venus, Earth, and Mars all have mountainous volcanoes, but those on Mars are the largest. Mars is smaller than Earth or Venus, so it has weaker gravity that lets mountains build up higher. In addition, its crust does not move about, so volcanic eruptions tend to happen again and again in the same place, with each lava flow piling on top of the last. Mars has the highest volcano in the solar system, Olympus Mons.

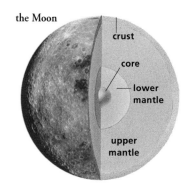

the Moon
- crust
- core
- lower mantle
- upper mantle

Earth's moon has no atmosphere.

Olympus Mons, Mars, 16 miles (25 km) high

Maxwell Montes, Venus, 7 miles (12 km) high

Mauna Kea, Hawaii, Earth, 5 miles (9 km) high from the sea bed

Earth's sea level

MERCURY

The smallest planet in the solar system after Pluto, Mercury is also the closest to the Sun. This means that it orbits the Sun much faster than any other planet does. But it spins relatively slowly. Mercury takes almost 59 of our days to spin once. It spins only three times for every two journeys it makes around the Sun. This has a very strange effect on the length of its day. If you landed on Mercury, you would find that two Mercury years pass between one sunrise and the next.

Mercury is one of the most cratered objects in the solar system. Its surface was shaped mainly by impacts and volcanic eruptions. Some time after most of the craters were formed, Mercury shrank a little as its surface cooled, making its crust wrinkle up in places.

△ **Mercury's surface**
Smothered in craters, Mercury looks very like Earth's moon. This picture is made from some of the 10,000 images taken by the *Mariner 10* spacecraft in 1974 and 1975.

▷ **Caloris Basin**
The "ripples" spreading out from the top of this picture are part of the largest impact scar on Mercury. Called the Caloris Basin, it is 800 miles (1,300 km) across and ringed by mountains a mile (1.6 km) high.

A BAKED PLANET

Mercury has no real atmosphere because it is baking hot and because the gravity of this small planet is too weak to hold on to much gas. If Mercury once had an atmosphere, it would have boiled away long ago under the blazing heat of the nearby Sun. Today the planet only has tiny amounts of gas, mainly given off by its hot rocks. It has daytime temperatures above 750°F (400°C), which is hot enough to melt tin and lead. At night, the temperature plunges below –290°F (–180°C).

IMPACT CRATERS

Crater formation
1 The circular craters on the surfaces of planets and moons were mostly formed when an object such as a comet or large meteorite (a rock from space) slammed into the surface. **2** The shock of an impact causes the object to explode like a bomb going off. **3** Shattered pieces of rock are flung upward out of the crater. **4** The shower of rock falls back, some of it into the crater and some building up the circular wall around it.

MERCURY	FACT	FILE

 Diameter at equator: 3,031 miles (4,878 km)

 Time taken to spin once: 58.65 Earth days

Mass (the amount of matter it contains): 0.055 of Earth's mass

Tilt of axis on which it spins: 0 degrees

Volume (the amount of space it takes up): 0.056 of Earth's volume

 Temperature of surface: 297°F (–183°C) to 800°F (427°C)

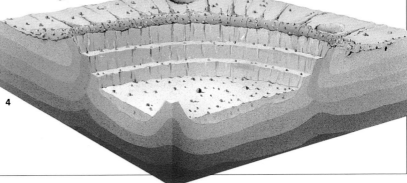

A cloudy atmosphere
This image made by the *Pioneer Venus* spacecraft in 1978 shows thick, swirling clouds at the top of Venus's atmosphere. The clouds are 20 miles (30 km) thick and are mainly made of drops of acid. They hide Venus's surface from our view.

VENUS– THE HOTHOUSE

Coming within 28 million miles (45 million kilometers) of Earth, Venus gets closer than any other planet. Its clouds reflect sunlight strongly, making it look very bright, so it is by far the easiest planet to spot in our sky. For a few weeks every seven months it is the brightest object in the evening sky to the west. When it is in the west, people call it the "evening star." About three and a half months later it appears in the eastern sky before sunrise. Then it is called the "morning star."

Venus is the second planet from the Sun, and it is only a little smaller than Earth. It takes 243 Earth days for Venus to spin once, giving it the longest "day" of any planet in the solar system.

A CHOKING ATMOSPHERE AND VOLCANIC SURFACE

Venus has an extremely hot and dry atmosphere which contains about 100 times as much gas as Earth's atmosphere. On Venus the atmospheric pressure (the weight of the atmosphere pressing down on the planet's surface) is about 90 times greater than on Earth. The atmosphere is mainly made of carbon dioxide, a gas that traps the heat from the Sun, keeping the surface temperature on Venus at a blistering 900°F (480°C).

In spite of the thick atmosphere, there is hardly any wind to wear away the mountains, volcanoes, and craters, so these have not changed in appearance since they formed millions of years ago. Venus has hundreds of thousands of volcanoes. A few are very large, but most are about 2 miles (3 kilometers) across and 300 feet (90 meters) high. Venus's thin, rocky skin floats on hot molten rock, which bursts out wherever it can.

The volcanic surface has been battered by meteorites. There are very few craters smaller than about 6 miles (10 kilometers) across because the smaller rocks were affected by Venus's atmosphere. Some "bounced off;" others slowed down or burned up in the thick atmosphere before they struck the surface. But even the larger craters are not as common as they are on the Moon or Mercury. This is because many of the craters that were made by large rocks crashing around when the solar system first formed have since been covered by flows of volcanic lava.

Venus has been visited by 23 spacecraft. Russian space scientists landed eight of these on the surface. The spacecraft were able to send back pictures of their surroundings and take samples of the rocks before their instruments gave out under the tremendous heat and pressure.

VENUS FACT FILE

Diameter at equator:
7,521 miles
(12,104 km)

Time taken to spin once:
243.16 Earth days

Mass (the amount of matter it contains):
0.815 of Earth's mass

Tilt of axis on which it spins: 178 degrees

Volume (the amount of space it takes up):
0.86 of Earth's volume

Average temperature:
cloud tops: –27°F (–33°C)
surface: 900°F (480°C)

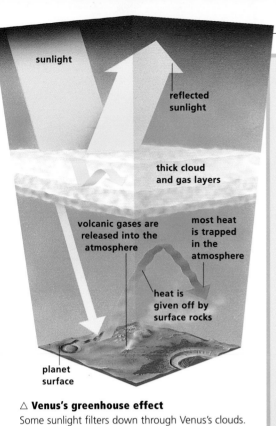

sunlight

reflected sunlight

thick cloud and gas layers

volcanic gases are released into the atmosphere

most heat is trapped in the atmosphere

heat is given off by surface rocks

planet surface

△ Venus's greenhouse effect

Some sunlight filters down through Venus's clouds. It warms up the atmosphere and the surface rocks. Most of the heat given off by the rocks cannot leak back into space because the atmosphere acts like a thick blanket. This keeps Venus's surface temperature very high.

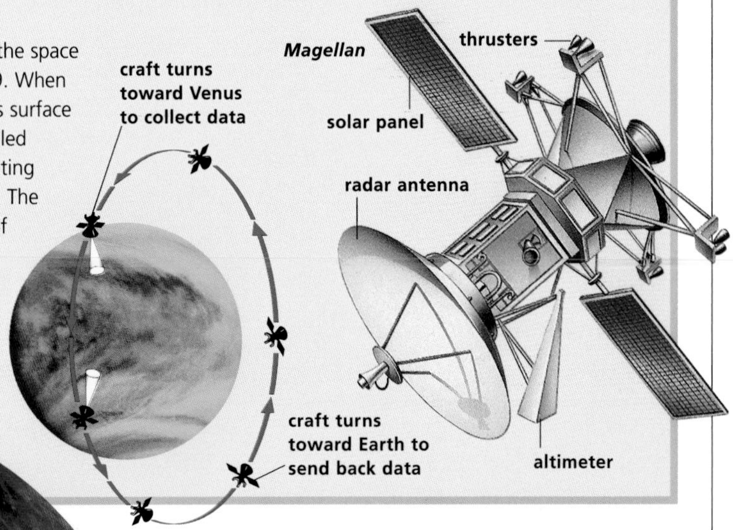

▷ A Magellan map

This global view of half of Venus was made by the *Magellan* spacecraft. The color coding shows highland and mountain regions in yellow, while low-lying plains are orange and brown.

THE MAGELLAN MISSION

Because Venus's surface is hidden from our view by clouds, the *Magellan* spacecraft was sent into orbit around the planet to make a map of its surface using radar. Radar uses radio waves, which easily go through clouds. *Magellan* bounced radar pulses off the surface of Venus and beamed the reflected pulses back to Earth. From these, a computer worked out what Venus's surface must look like. Each time *Magellan* circled the planet, it mapped a strip 15 miles (24 kilometers) wide and 6,000 miles (10,000 kilometers) long. It took three years to build up a complete picture of the world beneath the clouds. The spacecraft was named after the 16th-century Portuguese explorer, Ferdinand Magellan.

Mapping the surface

Magellan was launched on the space shuttle *Atlantis* in May 1989. When *Magellan* was above Venus's surface in its orbit, small gas jets called thrusters kept the craft pointing straight down at the planet. The radar antenna fired pulses of radio waves at Venus and picked up the reflections. The altimeter measured *Magellan*'s height above the planet's surface.

craft turns toward Venus to collect data

craft turns toward Earth to send back data

Magellan

thrusters

solar panel

radar antenna

altimeter

FEATURES OF THE SURFACE

▽ Craters, volcanoes, and mountains

Volcanoes are common on Venus. Repeated lava flows built up shield volcanoes, while the pancake-shaped dome volcanoes (which are unique to Venus) were made by single eruptions of very sticky lava. Folded mountains rose where the planet's crust moved and got squeezed. The planet also has nearly 900 impact craters, ranging from 1 to 150 miles (1.6 to 250 km) across.

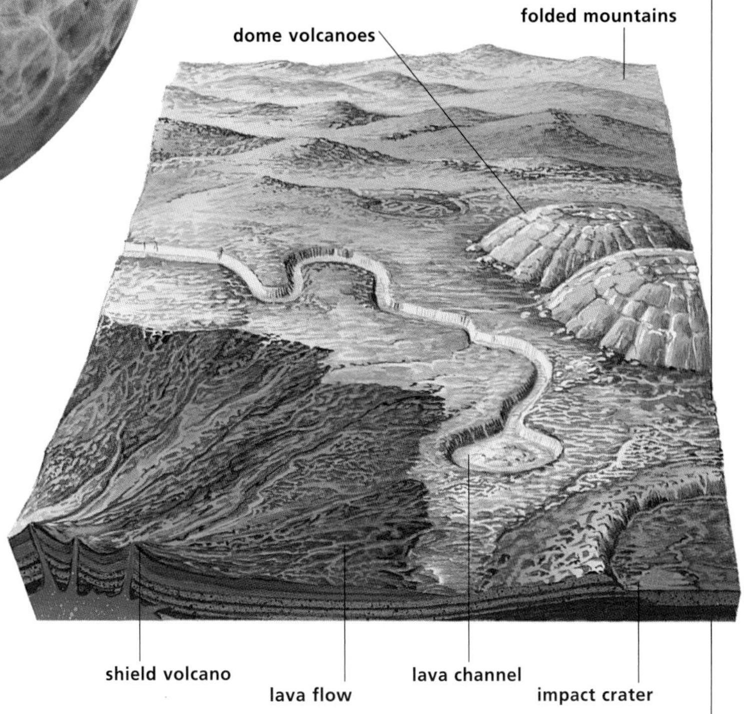

◁ On Venus's surface

This picture of Venus's surface was created by computer from the radar maps made by *Magellan*, such as the one pictured above. The taller mountain in the picture is Gula Mons, which is 2 miles (3 km) high. All over Venus, great lava flows stretch in every direction. The volcanoes have also blown out clouds of acid into the atmosphere.

dome volcanoes

folded mountains

shield volcano

lava flow

lava channel

impact crater

35

EARTH–THE LIVING PLANET

The planet on which we live, Earth has a thick atmosphere and huge supplies of water to form rivers, vast oceans, and clouds. The atmosphere acts like a blanket keeping the planet warm. It raises the temperature at the surface by 54°F (30°C). Without the atmosphere, Earth would be so cold that its oceans would be frozen. Earth is the only planet with liquid water at the surface and, as far as we know, it is the only place in the universe where there is life. Heat and light from the Sun, together with water, make most life on Earth possible. Over billions of years, life has changed the planet into a world where large animals, including humans, can live.

CARL SAGAN

The American astronomer Carl Sagan (1934–1996) was an expert on the atmospheres of planets. He studied how life might have started and developed on Earth. He was particularly interested in the possibility that life might also exist on other planets. Sagan had the idea of putting a plaque carrying a message from Earth on the *Pioneer 10* spacecraft, which flew past Jupiter in 1973 then on to the edge of the solar system and out into deep space. An identical plaque went on *Pioneer 11* the next year.

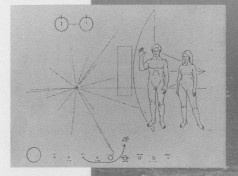

Carl Sagan *(top)* and the message about Earth *(right)* that was carried into space on *Pioneer 10* and *Pioneer 11*

A HABITABLE PLANET

Earth had an atmosphere soon after it formed but it did not contain oxygen as it does today. The atmosphere was made of carbon dioxide, water vapor, and nitrogen released from volcanoes. Gradually Earth cooled and the water vapor turned to rain. The rain eventually became the oceans that cover three-quarters of Earth's surface today. The first tiny forms of life began in the oceans about four billion years ago.

Water can hold carbon dioxide gas. Sea creatures use it to help make their shells. The early life in the seas used up a lot of carbon dioxide. The first green plants also used carbon dioxide and put oxygen into the air. By about two billion years ago, sea animals and plant life had removed nearly all the carbon dioxide from the air and produced large amounts of oxygen. If they had not, the carbon dioxide would cause Earth to be boiling hot, rather like Venus, and we would not have oxygen to breathe. About 30 miles (50 kilometers) above Earth's surface, a special kind of oxygen called ozone blocks out harmful rays from the Sun.

Air and water
The air on Earth is constantly on the move, creating winds and storms *(see above right)*. The pull of gravity from the Moon and the Sun cause the tides, which raise and lower the sea level twice a day. When there is a big storm at high tide, strong winds whip up giant waves and send them crashing to the shore with destructive force.

◁ ▽ **Reshaping
the surface**
Earth's weather and its
liquid interior make it the most
changeable planet in the solar system.
Large storms *(left)* can cause massive floods,
moving billions of tons of rocks and soil. Flood
waters wear away the land quickly and carry soil and
rock into the oceans. More dramatic still are volcanoes
(below) and earthquakes caused by movements in the
plates of rock in Earth's crust. Volcanic eruptions build
new land from lava and ash, and pump steam, carbon
dioxide, and poisonous gases into the atmosphere.
Earthquakes shake the land, sometimes violently
enough to open huge cracks in the ground.

△ **From space**
A satellite image of Earth
shows cloud patterns in the layer
of atmosphere that surrounds the
planet. Today, the atmosphere is
made mostly of nitrogen. Because
the Earth is ball shaped and tilted
on its axis, some parts of its
surface are heated more by the
Sun than others. This creates
bands of warmer rising air and
cooler sinking air around the
planet, which make the clouds,
storms, and winds of our weather.

Inside the Earth is hot, sticky
liquid rock and iron, which is
always moving. The continents
and ocean floors of Earth's
surface lie on vast plates of
solid rock that float on the
liquid rock beneath. Their
slow movement, called
continental drift, causes large
sections of Earth's crust to crash
together. Where this happens,
huge ridges or mountain ranges, such
as the Rockies, are formed. Sometimes
the plates tear apart, sinking enormous
trenches over great distances.

THE "LIFE ZONE"

Many living things have successfully
developed on Earth because our planet is
special. It gets just the right amount of heat
from the Sun so most of its surface is
neither too hot nor too cold. All life
needs liquid water, but it would boil
away if Earth got too hot and the
oceans would freeze solid if Earth's
temperature dropped too low. The
most important influence on a
planet's temperature is its distance
from the Sun. Earth's orbit is in
the "life zone" around the Sun,
where liquid water can exist.

Not too hot; not too cold
Only Earth lies within the "life
zone," where the temperature allows
liquid water to exist. Venus and Mars
lie on the very edges of the zone.
Both had water when they first
formed but lost it long ago.

● Mars ◯ Earth ◯ Venus   Sun

too hot

"life zone"

too cold

EARTH FACT FILE

 Diameter at equator:
7,926 miles
(12,756 km)

**Tilt of axis on which
it spins:**
23.44 degrees

 **Time taken to
spin once:**
23.93 hours

 **Average surface
temperature:**
72°F (22°C)

THE MOON

Earth's closest neighbor in space, the Moon is the only other world that humans have visited. Astronauts felt only one-sixth their normal weight when they were on the Moon's surface because gravity there is much weaker than on Earth. It is too feeble even to stop gases escaping into space, so the Moon is a dead world. There is no air, no liquid water, and no weather to alter its surface. The mountains, craters, lava, and dust have hardly changed over billions of years. In the daytime, the temperature on the Moon gets higher than the boiling point of water. During the night, which lasts for 14 of our days, it plunges to –300°F (–185°C).

MOUNTAINS AND "SEAS"

Samples of Moon rock and soil were brought back to Earth by U.S. Apollo astronauts and by three Russian Luna probes. They show that the Moon formed about 4.6 billion years ago. Unlike on Earth, where some mountains are the youngest landforms, the mountains on the Moon are the oldest part of its surface we can see. After the mountains were formed, the Moon was battered by meteorites and asteroids. The largest punched right through the surface rocks to the interior,

△ A lunar crater

Apollo astronauts took this view of the crater Eratosthenes, which is 36 miles (58 km) across. Its walls have slumped down to form terraces. The Sun is low in the sky, and the crater walls are casting long deep shadows.

◁ Features on the Moon

With binoculars you can see craters, dark plains, and bright mountainous regions on the Moon. Some of the easiest features to find are shown on this picture of the side of the Moon that faces Earth. Most lunar craters are named for famous astronomers or other scientists.

Moon map labels: SEA OF COLD, Plato, Jura mountains, SEA OF RAINS, Archimedes, Aristarchus, OCEAN OF STORMS, Kepler, Grimaldi, Eratosthenes, Copernicus, Apennine mountains, SEA OF VAPORS, SEA OF SERENITY, SEA OF TRANQUILITY, SEA OF CRISES, SEA OF FERTILITY, Langrenus, Theophilus, SEA OF NECTAR, Ptolemaeus, Albategnius, Alphonsus, Arzachel, SEA OF CLOUDS, SEA OF MOISTURE, Tycho

APOLLO MISSIONS TO THE MOON

The Moon landings

Six Apollo spacecraft each landed two astronauts on the Moon between 1969 and 1972. The spacecraft were launched from Earth on mighty Saturn V rockets, and had three main parts: the Command Module and Service Module (together known as the CSM), and the Lunar Module (LM).

1. The CSM, with three astronauts inside, separated from the Saturn V rocket, turned around, and docked onto the LM, which was carried on the rocket underneath the CSM.

part of Saturn V rocket

Lunar Module

Command Module (cone shape at top)

Service Module

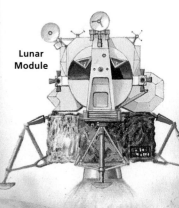

2. The CSM and LM went into orbit around the Moon. The LM with two astronauts inside separated from the CSM. The third astronaut stayed on board the orbiting CSM.

3. The LM fired rocket engines to slow it down as it fell toward the Moon's surface.

Lunar Module

which was then liquid. Warm lava gushed out to cover large lowland areas of the surface. Astronomers named the newer dark, flat areas *maria*, which is the Latin word for "seas," though they are now solid rock. Volcanic activity on the Moon stopped about three billion years ago. The Moon has now cooled and become almost completely solid inside. The Moon always keeps the same face to Earth, but photographs taken from spacecraft show that most of the side we cannot see is covered by cratered mountains.

DUST AND CRATERS

Astronauts found that the Moon's surface is covered in crunchy dust. Every time a meteorite hits the Moon, it smashes a patch of the surface into even finer dust. Impacts made all the craters we see on the Moon. A few are very large. Tycho is 53 miles (85 kilometers) across and has a peak in the center 7,500 feet (2.3 kilometers) high. Copernicus is 58 miles (93 kilometers) wide. Both these craters have bright rays around them where debris was scattered over a huge area. The largest crater, called Bailly, measures 183 miles (295 kilometers). Smaller craters are much more common. The Moon has probably gained three or four new craters, each about a mile (1.6 km) across, within the last million years.

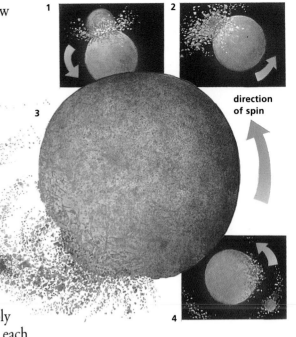

direction of spin

Where did the Moon come from?
Soon after Earth formed, it may have been struck by another rocky planet as large as Mars (1). Using supercomputers, astronomers have shown what might have happened. Rocks from Earth's outer layers and from the object that hit it were smashed into a great plume of debris (2 and 3). Some of the pieces clumped together to make the Moon (4).

The lunar surface
An astronaut takes samples of rock during the Apollo 17 mission. The Lunar Roving Vehicle (in the center) was used for traveling around. The sky is black even though it is day because there is no atmosphere to scatter sunlight and create a bright, colored sky.

4. To leave the Moon, the astronauts blasted back into orbit in the top half of the LM.

Command Module

Service Module

5. The LM docked with the CSM, which took all three astronauts back to Earth.

6. The Command Module containing the astronauts separated from the Service Module just before entering Earth's atmosphere. It landed in the ocean as planned.

Command Module

MOON FACT FILE

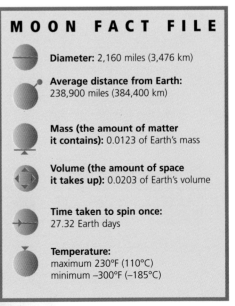

Diameter: 2,160 miles (3,476 km)

Average distance from Earth: 238,900 miles (384,400 km)

Mass (the amount of matter it contains): 0.0123 of Earth's mass

Volume (the amount of space it takes up): 0.0203 of Earth's volume

Time taken to spin once: 27.32 Earth days

Temperature: maximum 230°F (110°C) minimum –300°F (–185°C)

MARS–THE RED PLANET

In many ways, Mars is the planet most like our own, though it is only half as large. Wispy clouds and patches of mist form in its thin atmosphere, and winds raise billows of dust over its desertlike landscape. With its axis tilted at about the same angle as Earth's, Mars has similar, though longer, seasons. The martian day, called a "sol," is only a little over 24 hours long. Ice permanently caps the two poles, which grow and shrink with the seasons. But unlike Earth, Mars has no seas or rivers. The very low temperatures and thin atmosphere make it impossible for liquid water to exist there.

ice clouds

dust clouds

Weather on Mars
The *Hubble Space Telescope* took these pictures of Mars on July 9, 10, and 11, 1997. They show changing clouds of ice crystals near the north pole, and dust clouds just north of *Mars Pathfinder's* landing site, which is marked in each picture by a green cross.

A DRY, LIFELESS PLACE

Heavily cratered highlands cover most of Mars's southern hemisphere. Over the rest of its surface are plains of volcanic lava with fewer craters. In one region, called Tharsis, four huge extinct volcanoes top a great bulge in Mars's surface. When this bulge swelled up, it opened a deep crack in the crust. Called the Mariner Valley, it is long enough to stretch across the United States.

Landing craft from the Viking and *Pathfinder* spacecraft returned pictures to Earth of Mars's surface. They showed landscapes littered with rocks and a layer of fine, reddish soil, which is rich in iron.

Dried-up water channels on Mars were carved out long ago by falling rain and gushing floods. The climate has changed dramatically since then. When Mars first formed, it must have had a thicker atmosphere, but gas gradually escaped into space because Mars's gravity is not very strong. As the atmosphere got thinner, the climate became colder and all the remaining water froze. It has not rained on Mars for about three billion years.

Mars is so cold in places that carbon dioxide in the atmosphere freezes into frosty crystals of dry ice.

△ **A scarred surface**
This global view of Mars was put together from many images taken by the orbiting Viking spacecraft between 1976 and 1980. The huge complex of the Mariner Valley stretches a quarter of the way around the planet.

MARS FACT FILE

Diameter at equator:
4,222 miles (6,794 km)

Time taken to spin once: 24.6 Earth hours

Mass (the amount of matter it contains):
0.107 of Earth's mass

Tilt of axis on which it spins: 27 degrees

Volume (the amount of space it takes up):
0.150 of Earth's volume

Average temperature of surface: –9°F (–23°C)

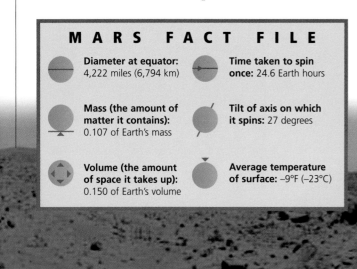

The temperature needs to fall below –190°F (–123°C) for this to happen. A coating of this dry ice over ordinary water ice causes the polar caps to spread in winter. Even in summer it is bitterly cold on Mars. The Viking landers found the temperature did not get above –27°F (–33°C).

The Viking landers carried out a number of experiments on the soil on Mars to look for signs of life— but found none. Even so, we cannot be sure yet that Mars does not have microscopic life somewhere—or perhaps did in the past when the planet was warmer and wetter.

PERCIVAL LOWELL

Fascinated by Mars, Percival Lowell (1855–1916), a wealthy businessman, set up his own observatory in Flagstaff, Arizona, specially to study the Red Planet. He believed he could see a network of lines criss-crossing Mars and thought that they were huge canals built by an intelligent civilization to carry water. Lowell's ideas caught on with the public. For many years people imagined Mars was probably inhabited. In 1897 the writer H. G. Wells based his story *War of the Worlds* on what Lowell had said about Mars. Today we know that the lines Lowell thought he saw were not really there.

Percival Lowell *(left)* and one of his maps of the "canals" he thought he saw on Mars *(above)*

◁ **Dried-up water channels on Mars**
Viking 1 landed in this area of Mars, called Chryse Planitia. The wavy, branching lines are channels cut by running water before about three billion years ago, when the climate on Mars was very different from today.

MOONS OF MARS

Mars has two tiny moons, Phobos and Deimos. They were discovered in 1877 and are probably asteroids that were captured by Mars's gravity. Phobos is the larger of the two and the nearer to Mars. It measures only 17 miles by 12 miles (28 by 20 km) and circles Mars in 7.6 hours. Deimos is 10 miles by 7 miles (16 by 12 km) and orbits Mars in 1.26 days.

Close-up pictures
Photographs of Mars's moons from the *Viking 2* spacecraft show they have uneven, cratered surfaces.

Phobos

Deimos

▽ **The Mars Pathfinder mission**
In July 1997, the spacecraft *Pathfinder* landed on Mars. Its fall was cushioned by large airbags rather like giant balloons. A TV camera carried on the craft took these views around its landing place. A miniature "rover" named Sojourner *(inset right)* was on board *Pathfinder*. Controllers on Earth moved Sojourner slowly around the planet's surface near the lander. It carried instruments to study the rocks.

ASTEROIDS–THE MINI PLANETS

Gaspra

As well as the major planets, thousands of small rocky chunks orbit the Sun. These are the asteroids, or minor planets. They are all too faint to be seen without a telescope. Ceres was the first to be discovered and is by far the largest. It was found in 1801, and its diameter is 605 miles (975 kilometers). The smallest asteroids are boulders less than a mile across. Most asteroids circle the Sun in a zone between the orbits of Mars and Jupiter called the asteroid belt. A few have been disturbed out of the asteroid belt and follow paths that are unusually elongated ellipses. Some of these can pass very close to Earth.

Mathilde

NEAR

Ida

△ **The NEAR mission and asteroid Mathilde**
The asteroid Eros is the main target of the Near-Earth Asteroid Rendezvous (NEAR) mission but, on its way, *NEAR* passed close by another asteroid, Mathilde, and sent back pictures. Mathilde is made of dark rock and is about 32 miles (52 km) across.

Dactyl

Gaspra, Ida, and Dactyl
On its way to Jupiter, the spacecraft *Galileo* passed close by two asteroids, Gaspra (*pictured top left*) in 1991 and Ida (*left*) in 1993. The fly-by of Ida revealed that it has a tiny moon, which was named Dactyl (*above*). Ida is 35 miles (56 km) long while Dactyl is less than 1 mile (1.6 km) across. Gaspra is 9 miles (15 km) long.

BODIES OF ROCK AND METAL

The asteroids are small bodies left over from when the solar system formed. All of them together contain less than one thousandth the amount of material in planet Earth. The next largest after Ceres are Pallas and Vesta, with diameters of just over 310 miles (about 500 kilometers). Then there are about 15 larger than 150 miles (240 kilometers) across. Spacecraft have taken close-up pictures of three smallish asteroids—Gaspra, Ida, and Mathilde. They are uneven-shaped rocks pitted by craters where smaller rocks have collided with them.

Asteroids are not all made of the same material. Most are very dark and dull, but others are shiny. Some are light-colored rock, and a few—the shiniest of all—are made mainly of metal. The metal probably came from the core of a very small planet that formed in the asteroid belt and was then smashed apart again.

An asteroid speeding close by Earth can for a short time become the closest natural object to our planet. In 1994, a small rock about 30 feet (10 meters) across passed only 65,000 miles (105,000 kilometers) away—less than one third the distance to the Moon.

One of the most unusual asteroids is in the outer solar system. Chiron, discovered in 1977, is on a path that takes it between the orbits of Jupiter and Uranus. In 1988 astronomers were surprised when it suddenly became much brighter. Closer observation showed it was surrounded by a cloud of gas and dust that had come off its surface, making it look like the bright coma of a comet. Asteroids and comets are very similar in many ways, except that comets have a lot of ice. Chiron seems to be halfway between a comet and an asteroid. Several other asteroids have been found in orbits similar to Chiron's. As a group they are called the Centaurs. However, none of the others has grown brighter like Chiron.

MYSTERIOUS VESTA

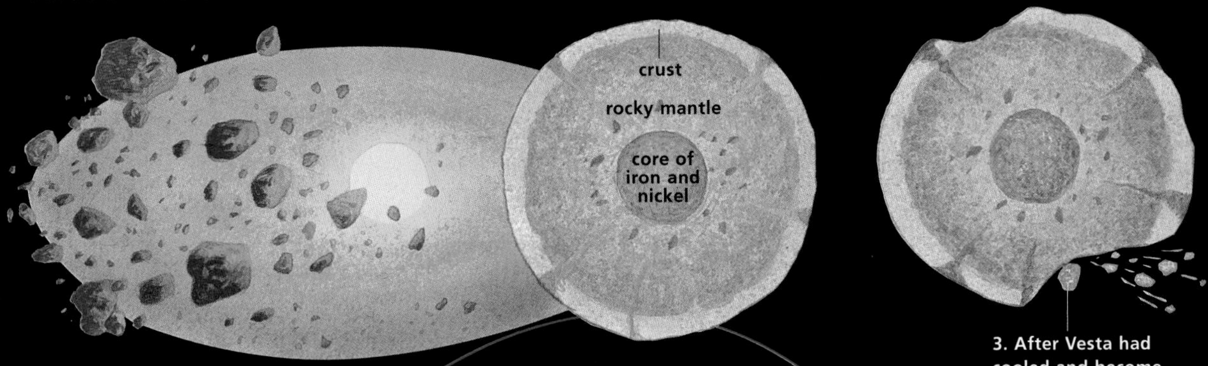

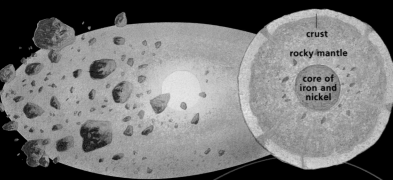

crust

rocky mantle

core of iron and nickel

1. As the solar system formed, small chunks of material collected together to make asteroid Vesta and it became hot.

2. Molton iron and nickel sank to the center of the hot asteroid. Lava from the interior flowed out through the crust onto the surface.

3. After Vesta had cooled and become solid, other rocks crashed onto the surface and dug out large craters in the crust revealing the mantle underneath.

◁ **Understanding asteroid Vesta**

Vesta is only 325 miles (525 km) across but looks like a tiny version of a rocky planet. It has a core, a mantle, and a crust. There are lava flows on its surface where liquid rock seeped out long ago when Vesta was hot. Some of the pieces that chipped off Vesta when other rocks crashed into it have traveled through the solar system and fallen to Earth as meteorites.

a computer image of Vesta made from observations by the *Hubble Space Telescope*

ASTEROID ORBITS

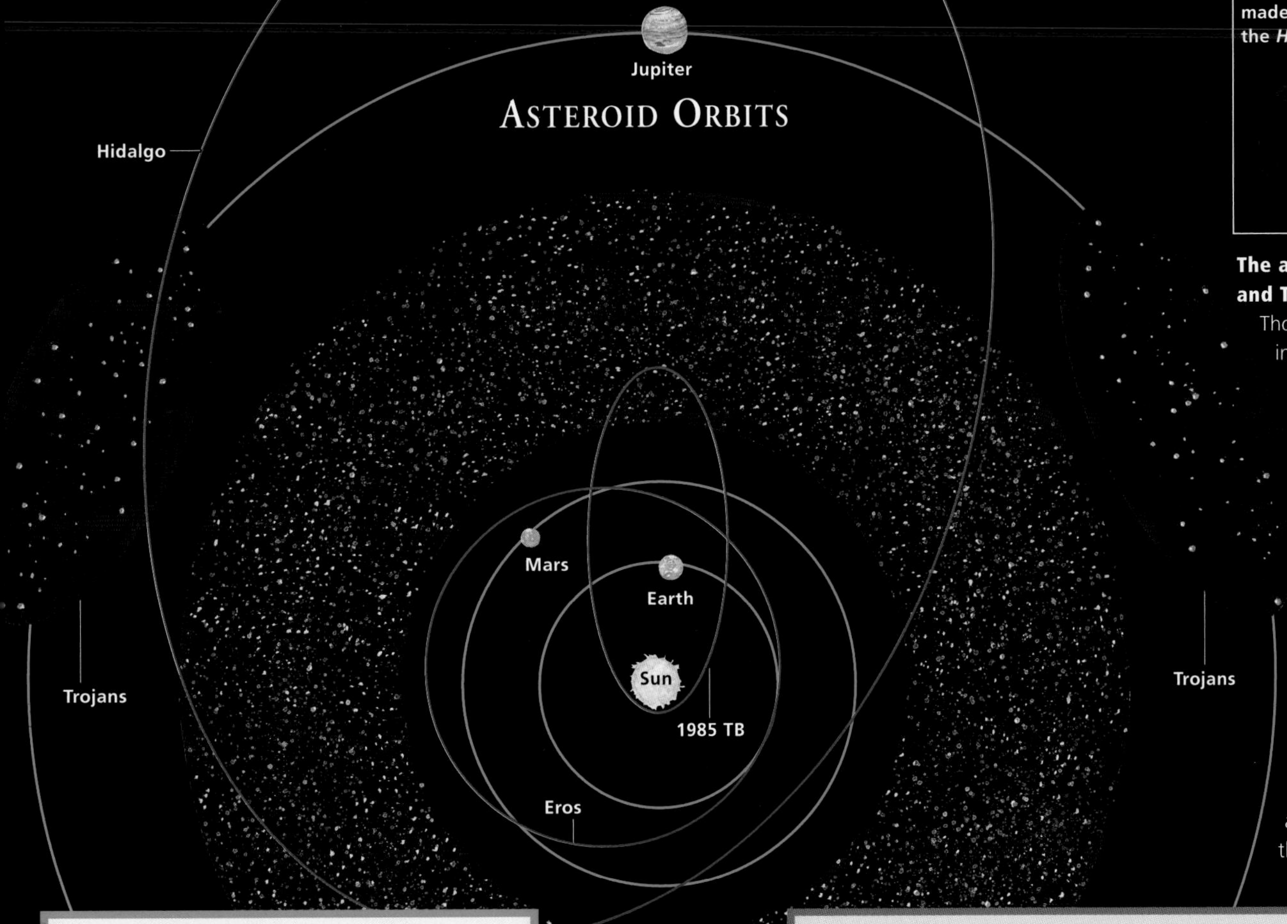

Jupiter

Hidalgo

Trojans

Mars

Earth

Sun

1985 TB

Eros

Trojans

asteroid belt

The asteroid belt and Trojans

Though most asteroids are in the main belt, there are exceptions. Several hundred, known as the Trojan asteroids, share Jupiter's orbit, clustered in two groups. Some asteroids, such as Eros, are closer to the Sun than the main belt, and some, such as 1985 TB, can even cut across Earth's orbit. Hidalgo follows a very elongated path that takes it from the asteroid belt out beyond the orbit of Saturn.

CHIRON'S ORBIT

Asteroid Chiron is one of several asteroids called the Centaurs, which follow paths between the orbits of Jupiter and Uranus.

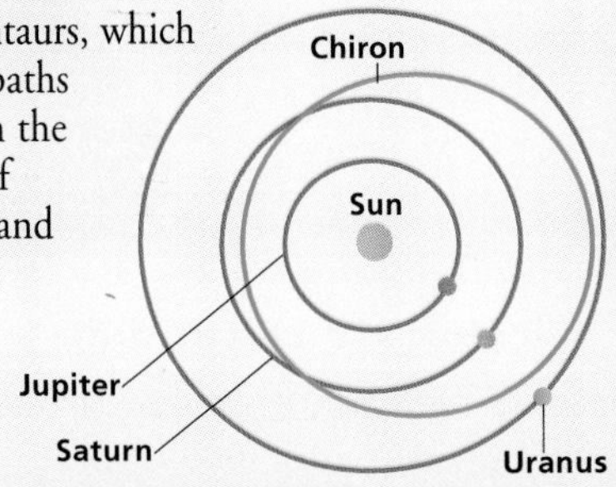

Chiron

Sun

Jupiter

Saturn

Uranus

ASTEROID FACT FILE

THE LARGEST ASTEROIDS			
Name	**Year discovered**	**Approximate average diameter**	**Distance from Sun (Earth = 1)**
Ceres	1801	605 miles (975 km)	2.77
Pallas	1802	330 miles (535 km)	2.77
Vesta	1807	325 miles (525 km)	2.36
Hygeia	1849	265 miles (425 km)	3.14
Davida	1903	200 miles (325 km)	3.18
Interamnia	1910	200 miles (325 km)	3.06
Cybele	1861	175 miles (280 km)	3.43
Europa	1858	175 miles (280 km)	3.10
Sylvia	1866	170 miles (270 km)	3.49
Patientia	1899	170 miles (270 km)	3.06

THE GIANT PLANETS

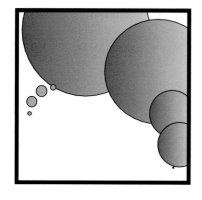

The four enormous planets in the outer solar system are very different from the rocky planets nearer the Sun. They are called the "gas giants" because the material they are made from includes vast amounts of hydrogen and helium, the main gases that make up the Sun. Beneath their clouds, there is no solid surface, so it will never be possible for spacecraft to land on these planets. If you could make a journey down into Jupiter, you would feel the gas getting thicker and thicker, and pressing in on you like a tremendously heavy weight. When you reached about 600 miles (1,000 kilometers) down, you would find the gas is squashed together so much it is turning into a liquid. Most of Jupiter is an incredible ocean of liquid hydrogen.

Which planets are gas giants?
Jupiter, Saturn, Uranus, and Neptune (shown in red) are large gassy planets in the outer solar system. Unlike any of the rocky planets, all four have ring systems and large families of moons.

COMPARING THE GIANT PLANETS

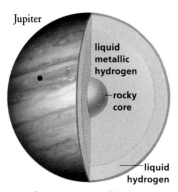

Jupiter

liquid metallic hydrogen

rocky core

liquid hydrogen

Most of Jupiter consists of hydrogen squashed under immense pressure into a form like a metallic liquid. Clouds of frozen crystals of ammonia, water, and other chemicals float in the atmosphere of hydrogen and helium.

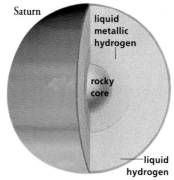

Saturn

liquid metallic hydrogen

rocky core

liquid hydrogen

Much of Saturn is liquid hydrogen. Deep inside there is some hydrogen in the form of a metallic liquid. Saturn's atmosphere and clouds are similar to Jupiter's, although the cloud patterns are not so complicated.

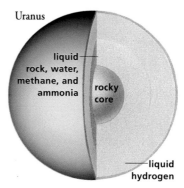

Uranus

liquid rock, water, methane, and ammonia

rocky core

liquid hydrogen

Around Uranus's rocky core there is a layer of a liquid chemical mixture topped by a layer of ordinary liquid hydrogen. The atmosphere contains a layer of methane clouds covered by haze.

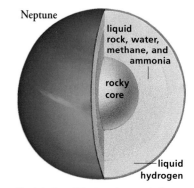

Neptune

liquid rock, water, methane, and ammonia

rocky core

liquid hydrogen

The interior of Neptune is very similar to Uranus, but heat rising from below creates changing patterns in the methane clouds. Bright clouds of frozen methane crystals form high in the atmosphere.

THE RING SYSTEMS

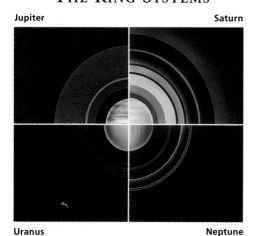

Jupiter   Saturn

Uranus   Neptune

Comparing the rings
Only Saturn's rings of shiny ice particles are broad and bright enough to be easily visible from Earth. Uranus and Neptune have narrow rings made of dark particles. Jupiter's rings are fine dust, rather like smoke. (To make it easier to compare the rings here, the planets have been drawn to the same size.)

INSIDE THE GIANTS

Saturn is similar to Jupiter. On the outside, both have layers of gas, making atmospheres with winds and clouds. But deep inside, the hydrogen is squashed down so much it takes on a form that conducts heat and electricity, like a molten metal. At their centers the gas giants have rocky cores about 12,500 miles (20,000 kilometers) across.

Uranus and Neptune have rocky cores about the same size as those of Jupiter and Saturn, but because Uranus and Neptune are smaller planets, they contain a much greater proportion of rocky material. Their blue color shows us that they are not made of exactly the same gases as Jupiter and Saturn. Uranus and Neptune have less hydrogen and more methane and ammonia.

HOW THE GIANT PLANETS GREW

When the solar system was forming, the giant planets grew much larger than the rocky planets nearer the Sun because they were in a colder place. The clumps of material collecting in the outer solar system included frozen, icy material, which became part of the giant planets. Closer to the Sun's heat, icy material evaporated away leaving only rock and metal to form the inner planets. With larger amounts of solid material to start with, the strong gravity of the growing giant planets was able to attract enormous amounts of gas, and to hang on to it.

Jupiter

THE VOYAGER MISSIONS

In 1977, two almost identical spacecraft, *Voyager 1* and *Voyager 2*, were launched to explore the outer solar system. They were a huge success and returned vast amounts of completely new information about the four giant planets, their rings, and moons. *Voyager 1* flew past Jupiter in 1979 and Saturn in 1980. On a different path, *Voyager 2* also skimmed past Jupiter and Saturn, in 1979 and 1981, but then went on to meet Uranus in 1986 and Neptune in 1989. *Voyager 2*'s space tour was possible only because the four giant planets were at suitable places in their orbits between 1979 and 1989. The giant planets form this pattern only once in about 175 years.

route of *Voyager 1*

route of *Voyager 2*

Voyagers' images of the giant planets
This is how the Voyager spacecraft saw the giant planets, which are shown here to scale. Saturn is more than four fifths the size of Jupiter. Uranus and Neptune are both about one third Jupiter's diameter. Two of Jupiter's moons are crossing the planet—Io on the left and Europa on the right.

Neptune

Saturn

Uranus

JUPITER–THE SUPERPLANET

Heavier than all the other planets of the solar system put together, Jupiter is also the largest. Alternate bands of light- and dark-colored clouds circle Jupiter, spread all around the planet by immensely strong winds. The Galileo probe into Jupiter's atmosphere measured wind speeds up to 400 miles (650 kilometers) per hour, which is many times faster than any winds on Earth. The winds are caused by Jupiter's rapid spin. One turn takes less than ten hours—the shortest "day" of any planet. Jupiter has at least 16 moons. They include the biggest moon in the solar system—Ganymede—which is larger than the planet Mercury. The *Voyager 1* spacecraft showed that Jupiter also has three rings, which are made of small amounts of dark dust.

Bands of clouds
The *Hubble Space Telescope* gave us this picture of Jupiter's cloud patterns. The dark spot is the shadow of Io, one of Jupiter's moons. Io itself is visible to the right of its shadow. The red and blue coloring around Jupiter is not real but due to the way the picture was made through colored filters.

The Galileo probe
In December 1995, a probe carried into space by the *Galileo* spacecraft slammed into Jupiter's atmosphere at more than 106,000 miles (170,000 km) per hour. A parachute slowed it down, then its six scientific instruments sent back information for 57 minutes while it descended through Jupiter's clouds.

WEATHER AND MAGNETISM

Although Jupiter has been cooling down since it formed 4.6 billion years ago, it is still very hot inside. The heat from inside causes gases in Jupiter's atmosphere to rise up. The gases fall again as they cool. Circling currents of gas form and make the cloud bands alternately light and dark. The light bands are rising gas topped by white clouds. Fewer clouds form over the belts where cool gas sinks down again. In these belts we are peering farther into Jupiter, and they look darker.

Details and colors in the cloud patterns are constantly changing, but the overall system of bands hardly alters. Jupiter's winds blow faster near the equator. Bands of clouds here

JUPITER FACT FILE

Diameter at equator:
88,846 miles
(142,984 km)

Time taken to spin once: 9.9 Earth hours

Mass (the amount of matter it contains):
318 times Earth's mass

Tilt of axis on which it spins: 3 degrees

Volume (the amount of space it takes up):
1,321 times Earth's volume

Temperature of cloud tops: –200°F (–130°C)

take five minutes less time to spin around once than the bands nearer the poles do.

A strong magnetic field surrounds Jupiter. Near the cloud tops, Jupiter's magnetism is 20 or 30 times stronger than Earth's, and it affects a vast region. The region around a planet where its magnetism is felt is called its magnetosphere. Jupiter's magnetosphere is huge—far larger even than the Sun—and it is a powerful source of radio waves.

The Great Red Spot
There are many oval spots on Jupiter, but the Great Red Spot is the largest. Two Earths could easily fit into it side by side. It is a kind of giant storm rotating counterclockwise. Observers first reported seeing it more than 300 years ago, but no one knows for sure why it is there or why it is red.

MOONS OF JUPITER

Jupiter's 16 moons divide into four groups. The four nearest Jupiter are tiny. Three of them were unknown until the Voyager missions. Next come the four large Galilean moons. Much farther out are two clusters of four small, dark moons. The farthest group travels around Jupiter backwards compared with the other moons. All eight outer moons have probably been captured by Jupiter's gravity. They may have come from two asteroids that broke into several pieces.

Each Galilean moon has its own character. Callisto is mostly ice and is heavily cratered. Part of Ganymede's icy surface is dark and cratered, but the rest is smoother where water once flooded out of cracks in the crust. Europa has less ice than Callisto and Ganymede; much of it has probably evaporated. Io is the most volcanic world in the solar system.

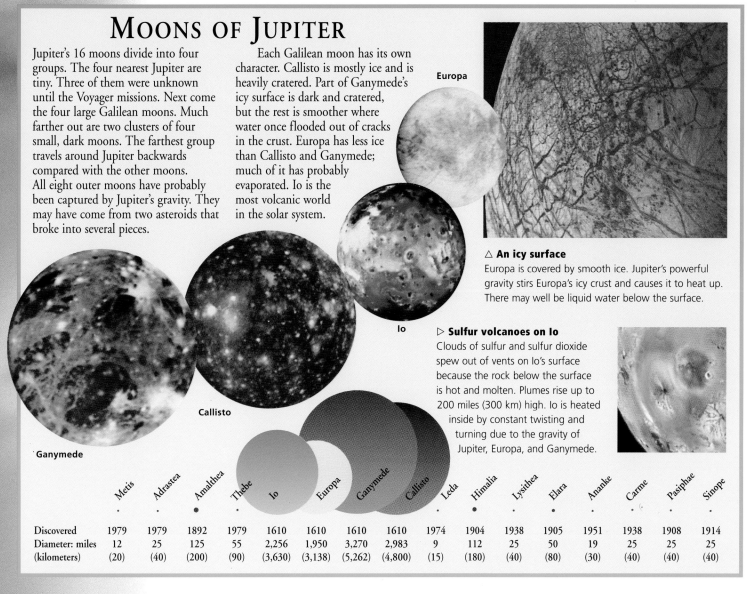

Europa

Io

Callisto

Ganymede

△ **An icy surface**
Europa is covered by smooth ice. Jupiter's powerful gravity stirs Europa's icy crust and causes it to heat up. There may well be liquid water below the surface.

▷ **Sulfur volcanoes on Io**
Clouds of sulfur and sulfur dioxide spew out of vents on Io's surface because the rock below the surface is hot and molten. Plumes rise up to 200 miles (300 km) high. Io is heated inside by constant twisting and turning due to the gravity of Jupiter, Europa, and Ganymede.

	Metis	Adrastea	Amalthea	Thebe	Io	Europa	Ganymede	Callisto	Leda	Himalia	Lysithea	Elara	Ananke	Carme	Pasiphae	Sinope
Discovered	1979	1979	1892	1979	1610	1610	1610	1610	1974	1904	1938	1905	1951	1938	1908	1914
Diameter: miles	12	25	125	55	2,256	1,950	3,270	2,983	9	112	25	50	19	25	25	25
(kilometers)	(20)	(40)	(200)	(90)	(3,630)	(3,138)	(5,262)	(4,800)	(15)	(180)	(40)	(80)	(30)	(40)	(40)	(40)

SATURN–THE RINGED PLANET

Surrounded by a spectacular set of rings, Saturn is one of the most beautiful sights visible through a telescope. Though the second largest planet and nearly as big as Jupiter, Saturn has less than one third Jupiter's mass. Material is spread so thinly in Saturn that the whole planet would float in water—if there were an ocean gigantic enough! Immensely strong winds on Saturn blow even harder than on Jupiter. Gusts whip around the equator more than ten times faster than hurricane-force winds on Earth.

CLOUDS AND STORMS

Saturn's yellowish cloud belts look fuzzier than the bands around Jupiter. The clouds form deeper in the atmosphere, and are underneath a layer of haze, which makes them harder to see. Most of the time, the cloud belts stay much the same but about every 30 years a giant storm causes a dramatic disturbance. Saturn takes 30 years to orbit the Sun, so it is likely that these giant storms are stirred up by seasonal changes in temperature. The last great storm was in 1990. Swirling white clouds spread around the planet until they stretched for more than ten times the size of Earth. Smaller storms can happen at any time, but they are also rare. All storms are thought to start where bubbles of warm gas rise up in the atmosphere. Like Jupiter, Saturn is hot inside.

Storms on Saturn
This *Hubble Space Telescope* picture was taken in 1994 and shows one of Saturn's rare storms. White clouds of frozen ammonia crystals formed over the storm area. Swept by thousand-mile- (1,600-km-) per-hour winds, the clouds make a shape rather like an arrowhead near the center of Saturn.

SATURN'S RINGS IN CLOSE-UP

Saturn
D ring
C ring
bright B ring
A ring

the Cassini division is a gap filled with faint ringlets

the narrow F ring is kept in line by the effects of gravity of two "shepherd" moons, Prometheus and Pandora

G ring

E ring

△ **Tilting rings**
Our view of Saturn's rings changes as the planet travels around the Sun. They are normally easy to see with a small telescope, but every 15 years they seem to close up then open out again. When they are exactly edge-on to us *(middle)*, we cannot see them.

SATURN FACT FILE

Diameter at equator:
74,897 miles
(120,536 km)

Time taken to spin once:
10.5 Earth hours

Mass (the amount of matter it contains):
95 times Earth's mass

Tilt of axis on which it spins: 27 degrees

Volume (the amount of space it takes up:
764 times Earth's volume

Temperature of cloud tops: −200°F (−130°C)

PATTERNS IN THE RINGS

In pictures the Voyager spacecraft took of Saturn's rings, you can see there are thousands of separate, narrow rings. The Voyager pictures also showed dark "spokes" that come and go across the rings. The spokes seem to be made of dust, which is lined up in some way by Saturn's magnetism.

No one knows for sure where Saturn's rings came from. They could be the remains of a comet or moon that came too close and was torn apart by the gravity of the giant planet. Perhaps the material is left over from the time when Saturn and its moons first formed.

Rings of ice

Saturn's rings are made up of millions of individual moonlets. They are like dirty snowballs, mostly made of frozen water, with some dust and rock mixed in. The smallest chunks are about the size of a golf ball. A few of the largest may be half a mile (1 km) across.

MOONS OF SATURN

At least 18 moons keep Saturn company, and astronomers suspect there may be more. Each one is different, though all are made of a mixture of ice and rock. The largest, Titan, is bigger than the planet Mercury and is the only moon in the solar system with a thick atmosphere. The surfaces of Saturn's other moons are mostly dotted with craters, although many of the craters on Enceladus have been covered over by ice. The huge Herschel crater on Mimas was made by an impact that nearly shattered the whole moon. A massive canyon cuts three-quarters of the way around Tethys.

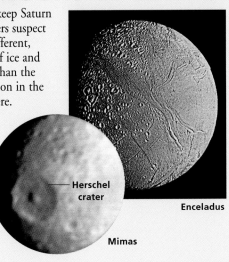

Herschel crater

Mimas

Enceladus

Titan

△ Visiting Titan

The atmosphere surrounding Titan is four times thicker than Earth's atmosphere and is mainly made of nitrogen. No one has ever seen Titan's surface because it is always hidden by orange-colored haze. In 2004, the *Cassini* spacecraft will release a probe that will parachute down onto Titan. The probe carries six instruments to send back pictures and data.

	Pan	Atlas	Prometheus	Pandora	Janus	Epimetheus	Mimas	Enceladus	Tethys	Telesto	Calypso	Dione	Helene	Rhea	Titan	Hyperion	Iapetus	Phoebe
Discovered	1985	1980	1980	1980	1966	1980	1789	1789	1684	1980	1980	1684	1980	1672	1655	1848	1671	1898
Diameter: miles	12	25	50	62	118	75	245	312	651	16	16	696	19	951	3,200	168	892	137
(kilometers)	(20)	(40)	(80)	(100)	(190)	(120)	(394)	(502)	(1,048)	(25)	(25)	(1,120)	(30)	(1,530)	(5,150)	(270)	(1,435)	(220)

URANUS AND NEPTUNE—THE BLUE PLANETS

WILLIAM HERSCHEL

Uranus was discovered by accident in 1781 by William Herschel (1738–1822) when he was studying stars with a telescope. It was the first planet to be found that could not be seen by the naked eye. Herschel was a professional musician from Hanover (now part of Germany) who settled in England. His hobby was building astronomical telescopes, and he was very skilled at observing. Finding Uranus made him world famous. His sister, Caroline Herschel (1750–1848), worked alongside him and discovered several comets.

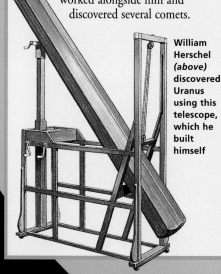

William Herschel (above) discovered Uranus using this telescope, which he built himself

The two distant giants of the solar system are similar in many ways. Both are about four times the size of Earth and are covered by thick, blue clouds. Their beautiful blue colors are an effect of the methane gas in their atmospheres. Both planets have ring systems and large families of moons. But the appearances of the two planets are quite different. Uranus looks nearly the same all over. Its bands of clouds are not very varied and are barely visible through a thick veil of haze that lies over the top of them. By contrast, Neptune is ever-changing. Huge, dark storm spots and flurries of bright clouds form and then disappear again.

URANUS

When *Voyager 2* flew past Uranus in 1986 it detected only very faint cloud markings. But in 1994 the *Hubble Space Telescope* spotted two large, bright clouds high up over the planet. The cloudiness probably varies with Uranus's strange seasons. Because of the way the planet is tilted, each pole on Uranus experiences 42 years when the Sun never sets, followed by 42 years of darkness!

Uranus's rings were discovered in 1977 when the planet's path crossed in front of a star. The star's brightness dipped and returned to normal several times before and after Uranus crossed in front of it. The only explanation was the existence of a set of rings that were crossing in front of the star, too. There are nine narrow rings made of individual particles as black as coal. They reflect so little sunlight that the rings are invisible from Earth's surface, but *Voyager 2* and the *Hubble Space Telescope* have taken pictures of them.

A tilted planet
Because the axis on which it spins is tilted right over, Uranus orbits the Sun lying on its side. In this *Hubble Space Telescope* picture, the hazy south pole is facing us.

Diameter at equator: 31,763 miles (51,118 km)

Mass (the amount of matter it contains): 14.5 times Earth's mass

Volume (the amount of space it takes up): 63 times Earth's volume

Time taken to spin once: 17.2 Earth hours

Tilt of axis on which it spins: 97.9 degrees

Temperature at cloud tops: −330°F (−200°C)

◁ **Neptune's clouds**
Bright, white clouds made of crystals of frozen methane gas form high up in Neptune's atmosphere. They float up to 31 miles (50 km) above the main blue cloud layers, and come and go over time.

NEPTUNE

Neptune was discovered in 1845 at the Berlin Observatory in Germany after two mathematicians, each working on his own, calculated where it would be found. Uranus was drifting slightly off the expected path of its orbit around the Sun. Urbain J. J. Leverrier in France and John Couch Adams in England both thought the gravity of an unknown planet was disturbing it. Both correctly worked out the new planet's position, but Leverrier won the race to get his prediction checked.

Neptune remained a mystery until *Voyager 2* flew close by in 1989. The spacecraft discovered violent weather. Winds around Neptune's equator blow at more than 1,250 miles (2,000 kilometers) per hour. They are the strongest winds known anywhere. *Voyager 2* also saw four thin, faint rings around Neptune, made of black dust.

Blurring by Earth's atmosphere makes it very difficult to see details of Neptune's clouds with telescopes on Earth. But since 1994, astronomers have used the *Hubble Space Telescope* to track the dramatic changes.

N E P T U N E   F A C T   F I L E

Diameter at equator:
30,778 miles
(49,532 km)

Time taken to spin once:
16.1 Earth hours

Mass (the amount of matter it contains):
17.2 times Earth's mass

Tilt of axis on which it spins: 29.6 degrees

Volume (the amount of space it takes up):
58 times Earth's volume

Temperature at cloud tops: –330°F (–200°C)

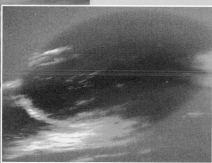

△ ▷ **Stormy weather**
In 1989, *Voyager 2* took pictures of a storm region on Neptune that was as big as Earth. It was called the Great Dark Spot *(above)*. When the *Hubble Space Telescope* was turned on Neptune in 1994, this storm had disappeared but a smaller one had started. The *HST* has followed the changing pattern of clouds on Neptune *(right)*.

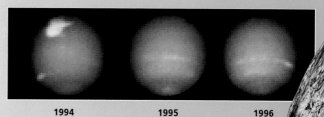

1994   **1995**   **1996**

MOONS OF URANUS AND NEPTUNE

Triton

The moons of these very cold, distant planets are made of a mixture of icy materials and rock. No two moons look the same, though they all have craters. *Voyager 2*'s close-ups of Uranus's five larger moons show long cracks and trenches. *Voyager 2* discovered ten new moons around Uranus, and six small, dark ones orbiting close to Neptune. Neptune's two outer moons have unusual orbits and were probably captured by the planet. Triton goes around backwards, and Nereid's orbit is a very stretched-out ellipse.

△ **Scarred Miranda**
There are so many different landscapes on the surface of Uranus's moon Miranda, it looks rather like patchwork.

▷ **Triton—Neptune's largest moon**
About the same size as Earth's moon, Triton has an icy surface, which is patterned with ridges, trenches, and craters. At –390°F (–235°C), it has the lowest measured temperature of a body in the solar system. *Voyager 2* discovered several places where plumes of gas, ice, and dust were erupting from below the surface and shooting up to 5 miles (8 km) high. Winds blowing in Triton's very thin atmosphere of nitrogen swept the plumes into long, dark streaks.

NEPTUNE'S MOONS

	Naiad	Thalassa	Despina	Galatea	Larissa	Proteus	Triton	Nereid
Discovered	1989	1989	1989	1989	1989	1989	1846	1949
Diameter: miles	34	50	112	93	119	258	1,681	149
(kilometers)	(54)	(80)	(180)	(150)	(192)	(416)	(2,705)	(240)

URANUS'S MOONS

	Cordelia	Ophelia	Bianca	Cressida	Desdemona	Juliet	Portia	Rosalind	Belinda	Puck	Miranda	Ariel	Umbriel	Titania	Oberon	S/1997 U2	S/1997 U1
Discovered	1986	1986	1986	1986	1986	1986	1986	1986	1986	1985	1948	1851	1851	1787	1787	1997	1997
Diameter: miles	16	19	26	39	34	52	67	34	41	96	293	720	726	980	946	100	50
(kilometers)	(26)	(30)	(42)	(62)	(54)	(84)	(108)	(54)	(66)	(154)	(472)	(1,158)	(1,169)	(1,578)	(1,523)	(160)	(80)

PLUTO, CHARON, AND THE ICE DWARFS

The smallest planet in the solar system is Pluto. Much of the time it is also the most distant planet. In 1978, astronomer James Christy noticed that Pluto looked pear-shaped on a photograph. He realized that Pluto has a moon. Called Charon, Pluto's moon is unusually large in relation to the size of its parent planet.

People used to wonder whether there might be another planet—"Planet X"—beyond Pluto. However, astronomers have now discovered that Pluto belongs to a whole family of icy dwarf planets orbiting the Sun beyond Neptune. There are probably thousands of them in what is called the Kuiper Belt, but it is unlikely that any are larger than Pluto.

THE SMALLEST PLANET AND ITS MOON

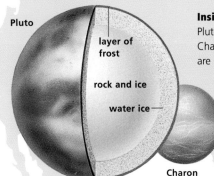

Pluto

layer of frost

rock and ice

water ice

Charon

Inside Pluto
Pluto is smaller than Earth's Moon and Charon is half the size of Pluto. Here, the two are compared in size with North and South America. No one is sure what Pluto is like inside. It is probably a mixture of ice and rock, covered with a mantle of water ice 125-200 miles (200-300 km) thick. On the surface, frozen methane, carbon monoxide, and nitrogen form a layer of frost, perhaps several miles or kilometers deep.

HST image of Pluto and Charon
In 1994, the _Hubble Space Telescope_ took the first image of Pluto _(bottom, with Charon at top)_ that shows up dark and light areas on its surface. The light patches include a bright cap on Pluto's pole, which is tilted over at an angle of 57 degrees.

DISCOVERING PLUTO

Clyde Tombaugh discovered Pluto in 1930. He had been working for about a year, searching for evidence of a distant planet moving against the background of stars. It was soon found that Pluto's orbit is much more elliptical than any other planet's, and it is tilted to the other planets' orbits by 17 degrees.

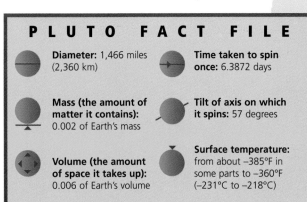

PLUTO FACT FILE

Diameter: 1,466 miles (2,360 km)

Time taken to spin once: 6.3872 days

Mass (the amount of matter it contains): 0.002 of Earth's mass

Tilt of axis on which it spins: 57 degrees

Volume (the amount of space it takes up): 0.006 of Earth's volume

Surface temperature: from about –385°F in some parts to –360°F (–231°C to –218°C)

But Pluto is so small and remote, we learned very little more about it until the 1970s, when frozen methane was found on its surface, and its moon, Charon, was discovered.

In 1988, Pluto crossed in front of a star. The star's light did not disappear suddenly, but dimmed gradually. That showed Pluto has a thin atmosphere.

When Pluto is nearest the Sun, its atmosphere gets thicker because the increase in warmth releases gases from the frost on the planet's surface. When Pluto's distance from the Sun increases, fresh, bright frost settles on the surface and the atmosphere becomes thinner.

This cycle of change causes Pluto's brightness to vary, and alters the pattern of dark and light areas on its surface.

CHARON AND FARTHER OUT

No features have been seen on Charon, but its surface is different from Pluto's. It is a different color, and it has frozen water but no methane. Astronomers have puzzled over how Pluto and Charon formed and came to be in orbit together. One idea is that a great collision took place early in the solar system's history. At that time there were probably far more icy dwarfs orbiting beyond Neptune. They were pieces left over after the giant planets had formed. Most of them ended up much farther out, in what is now the Oort Cloud.

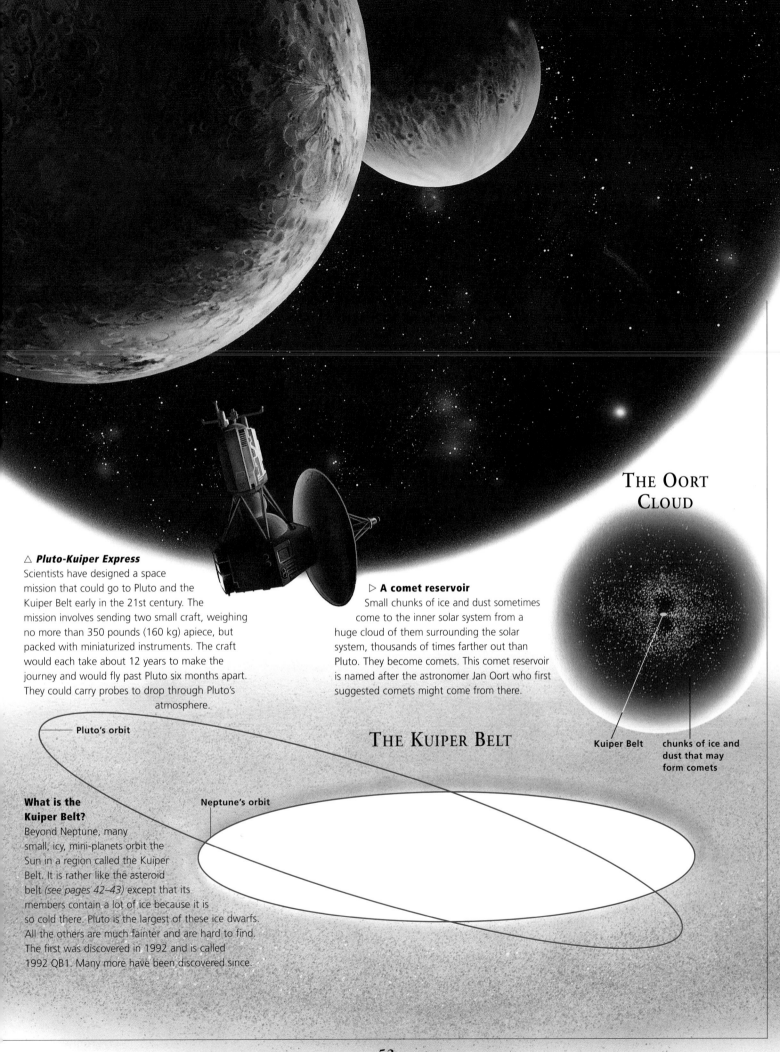

△ Pluto-Kuiper Express

Scientists have designed a space
mission that could go to Pluto and the
Kuiper Belt early in the 21st century. The
mission involves sending two small craft, weighing
no more than 350 pounds (160 kg) apiece, but
packed with miniaturized instruments. The craft
would each take about 12 years to make the
journey and would fly past Pluto six months apart.
They could carry probes to drop through Pluto's
atmosphere.

▷ A comet reservoir

Small chunks of ice and dust sometimes
come to the inner solar system from a
huge cloud of them surrounding the solar
system, thousands of times farther out than
Pluto. They become comets. This comet reservoir
is named after the astronomer Jan Oort who first
suggested comets might come from there.

THE OORT CLOUD

Kuiper Belt   chunks of ice and
dust that may
form comets

THE KUIPER BELT

Pluto's orbit

Neptune's orbit

What is the Kuiper Belt?

Beyond Neptune, many
small, icy, mini-planets orbit the
Sun in a region called the Kuiper
Belt. It is rather like the asteroid
belt (see pages 42–43) except that its
members contain a lot of ice because it is
so cold there. Pluto is the largest of these ice dwarfs.
All the others are much fainter and are hard to find.
The first was discovered in 1992 and is called
1992 QB1. Many more have been discovered since.

COMETS

A bright comet is one of the most spectacular objects in the night sky. About ten comets are discovered every year, but most of them are very faint. A comet that is easily visible to the naked eye typically appears once every ten to twenty years. Most bright comets turn up unexpectedly and are only seen once. But some come around regularly. The most famous and by far the brightest of these is Halley's Comet, which takes 76 years to orbit the Sun. It has been observed at every return for over 2,200 years. The last time was in 1986.

Comet Hale–Bopp
Millions of people around the world saw Comet Hale-Bopp in 1997. It was discovered by Alan Hale and Thomas Bopp on July 22, 1995, and became one of the brightest comets of the 20th century. Its nucleus was estimated to be 25 miles (40 km) across, twice as big as the nucleus of Halley's Comet.

HEADS AND TAILS

The head of a comet has a small, solid nucleus buried inside a huge cloud of gas and dust, called the coma. A nucleus with a diameter of 20 miles (32 kilometers) can give off a cloud of gas half a million miles (800,000 kilometers) across. The gas and the dust form separate tails, which grow longer as the comet gets nearer the Sun. They can be up to 50 million miles (80 million kilometers) long. Comet tails always stream away from the Sun. The gas is swept along by the solar wind *(see page 19)* while the dust particles are gently pushed by the effect of sunlight falling on them. A comet loses some of its material every time it passes around the Sun.

Although a comet becomes very large, it contains very little material. Earth has passed through the tail of a comet without any noticeable effect. Earth's closest encounter with a comet nucleus was in 1770, when Lexell's Comet came within 1.4 million miles (2.2 million kilometers). That comet has not been seen since.

Comets gradually move across the sky like planets. They are usually visible for a few weeks. New comets are normally named after their discoverer. Halley's Comet is one of the few exceptions. Edmond Halley realized that the comet he saw in 1682 was the same one that had been observed at least twice before—76 years earlier (in 1607) and 76 years before that (in 1531).

How comets get tails
When a comet nucleus is a long way from the Sun, it has no coma or tail. As it approaches the Sun, its surface temperature goes up and the ice within it starts to evaporate. Gas and dust are released and stream off the nucleus, creating a huge cloud that trails away from the Sun to give the comet two tails—a curved yellowish dust tail and a straight bluish gas tail.

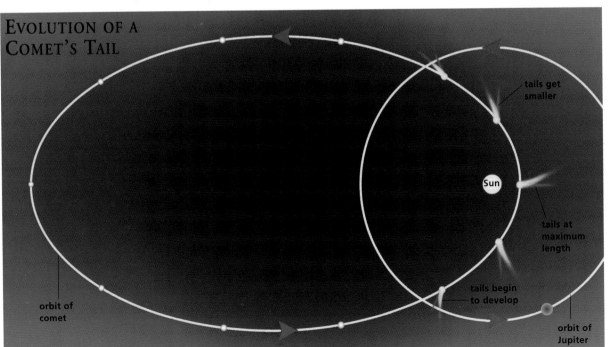

EVOLUTION OF A COMET'S TAIL

tails get smaller

Sun

tails at maximum length

tails begin to develop

orbit of comet

orbit of Jupiter

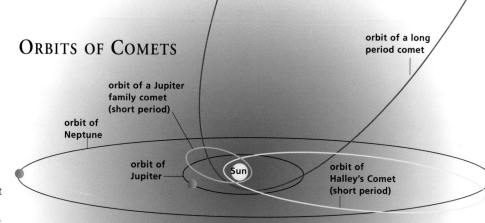

△ Comet Shoemaker–Levy 9 hits Jupiter

When Comet Shoemaker-Levy 9 was discovered in 1993, it was orbiting the planet Jupiter, which had captured the comet with its powerful gravity. During a close pass by Jupiter in 1992, the comet had broken into about 20 pieces *(above right)*. Astronomers predicted that these would fall into Jupiter the next time they swung near the planet. When the crashes happened, in July 1994, they caused hot flashes in Jupiter's atmosphere and left huge dark clouds that lasted several months *(above)*.

▷ Comets in orbit

Most comets travel to the inner solar system from about one light year away. They swing around the Sun then disappear far into space for thousands of years. These are called long period comets. If a comet passes close to a giant planet, particularly Jupiter, it can be caught in a smaller elliptical orbit and become a short period comet. Jupiter has trapped several dozen comets, known as Jupiter family comets, which take 5–11 years to orbit the Sun.

ORBITS OF COMETS

orbit of a long period comet

orbit of a Jupiter family comet (short period)

orbit of Neptune

orbit of Jupiter

Sun

orbit of Halley's Comet (short period)

△ Terrifying comets!

Throughout history and around the world, people believed that comets were signs of a coming disaster, probably because they appeared without warning and can be such an awesome sight in the sky.

GIOTTO

The spacecraft sent to explore Halley's Comet was named after the artist Giotto, who included the comet in a painting on the wall of a chapel in Padua, Italy, in 1303. He had seen the comet two years earlier. The spacecraft's camera and other instruments worked perfectly until two seconds before it passed closest to the comet nucleus in March 1986. Then dust hitting the craft put the camera out of action and cut off all contact with *Giotto* for a short time. In 1992, some of *Giotto*'s instruments were successfully turned on again to study another comet, called Grigg–Skjellerup.

GIOTTO

The nucleus of Halley's Comet

This close-up of the nucleus of Halley's Comet is made up of images from the *Giotto* spacecraft *(left)*. It shows gas and dust coming off the surface in jets on the side facing the Sun. The nucleus measures about 9 by 5 miles (15 by 8 km) and is mainly made of frozen water with tiny bits of dark solid material embedded in it. On the outside is a thin crust of this "dirt" making the nucleus as black as coal.

METEORS AND METEORITES

iron meteorite

Almost any dark, clear night, you might catch sight of the fiery trail of a "shooting star" whizzing across the sky. But this trail of light is not made by a star. It is called a meteor, and it is caused by a tiny speck of dust from space traveling at high speed into Earth's atmosphere, where it burns up some 55 miles (90 kilometers) above us. These particles of dust are usually the size of grains of sand, but are more crumbly than sand. Sometimes, larger chunks of material enter our atmosphere and survive the journey to the ground. Natural rocks from space that land on Earth are called meteorites.

WHERE DO THEY COME FROM?

Between the planets, space is strewn with bits of rocky material, ranging from microscopic dust particles to large boulders and stray asteroids. Earth is constantly bombarded by these pieces of natural space debris, which are called meteoroids. Meteoroids between the size of a sand grain and a pebble burn up completely in our atmosphere, but very fine dust and rocks larger than pebbles can reach the ground. Particles of very fine space dust are called micrometeorites, and Earth sweeps up about 10,000 tons of them every year. No one can be sure how many larger meteorites fall since most are never seen or found.

Small particles of dust from comets are responsible for regular meteor showers, when there are more meteors in the sky than on a normal night. Astronomers have now worked out which comets are responsible for many of the showers that are seen each year. For example, two showers come from Halley's Comet: the Orionids in October and the Eta Aquarids at the beginning of May.

Many meteorites seem to have come originally from the asteroid belt. Astronomers know this because these meteorites reflect sunlight in a way similar to asteroids. A small number of meteorites have been found that come from the Moon or from Mars. They were probably blasted out into space by some of the impacts that made craters on Mars and the Moon.

METEOR STREAMS

orbit of meteoroids

Earth's orbit

Sun

Earth

What are meteor streams?
Comets shed dust particles as they travel around the Sun. Eventually, a trail of dust is left around the whole of the comet's orbit, creating a meteor stream. If the stream crosses Earth's orbit, Earth passes through the dust at the same time each year, and we see an annual meteor shower.

The radiant of a meteor shower
The trails of meteors in a particular shower can all be traced back to one point in the sky, called the radiant. In fact, the dust particles enter Earth's atmosphere along parallel tracks but we see a perspective effect, just like looking along railroad tracks that seem to meet in the distance. A meteor shower is named for the constellation in which its radiant lies.

stony–iron meteorite

stony meteorite from Mars

▷ **Meteor Crater, Arizona**
A meteorite weighing more than 10,000 tons made this crater 4,000 feet (1,200 m) wide when it fell about 50,000 years ago in what is now Arizona. Most of it was destroyed in the explosion, but 18 tons of iron meteorite fragments have been found around the crater.

What are meteorites made of?
The three main types of meteorites are pictured above. Iron meteorites are made from iron and nickel. Criss-cross patterns of iron and nickel crystals show up when they are cut through and polished. More than 90 percent of meteorites are made of rock and are called stony meteorites. The one shown here has been identified as rock from Mars. About 1 percent of all meteorites are roughly half rock and half metal. They are called stony-iron meteorites.

Hoba West meteorite
The world's largest known meteorite is still where it was found in Namibia, Africa, in 1920. It has become a national monument. The weight of this iron meteorite is 120,000 pounds (55,000 kg).

WHEN METEORITES LAND
No one in recent history has been killed or seriously hurt by a meteorite, but there is evidence that some large meteorites fell to Earth in the distant past. Impact craters on our planet soon get worn away by wind and rain, but about 70 have now been discovered. The best preserved and the most famous (*pictured above*) is in Arizona.

When a meteorite comes in at high speed, there is an enormous explosion, which gouges out a crater and destroys most of the meteorite. A very large meteorite could have a devastating effect around the world, raising dust in the atmosphere and starting huge fires.

Some scientists think a giant meteorite hitting what is now Mexico caused the dinosaurs and many other animal species to die out on Earth about 65 million years ago.

Finding meteorites is not easy, unless someone happens to see one fall. Since 1969, the most important place in the world for meteorite hunters has been Antarctica. Thousands of meteorites have been collected there—more than in the whole of the rest of the world. They are carried along by the slowly moving ice so that many meteorites that fell long ago have accumulated in particular places, where they stand out against the white surface.

MAJOR METEOR SHOWERS

month name main dates	January **Quadrantids** January 3-4	month name main date	August **Perseids** August 12
month name main dates	May **Eta Aquarids** May 4-6	month name main date	October **Orionids** Oct 21
month name main dates	July/August **Delta Aquarids** July 29–Aug 6	month name main dates	December **Geminids** Dec 13-14

SKYWATCHING

Discovering the stars and planets for yourself is exciting and fun—and it is not hard to get started. You will be surprised at what you can see with just your eyes. But binoculars and telescopes show you even more.

The photograph *(left)* shows part of the concentration of stars that can be observed in the Milky Way.

STARTING ASTRONOMY

To see the stars well, you need to be away from city lights. In a brightly lit place you will be lucky to see more than a hundred stars, but you can see ten times as many from somewhere dark. When you first go out in the dark it is difficult to see anything except the brightest stars, but after about 20 minutes, your eyes become adapted and you can spot dimmer things. If you use a flashlight, choose one with a red light (or cover an ordinary flashlight with a red filter) to help keep your eyes adapted to the dark.

Castor
Pollux
GEMINI
the Pleiades
TAURUS
Aldebaran
ORION
Procyon **CANIS MINOR**
Betelgeuse
Rigel
Sirius
CANIS MAJOR
LEPUS
ERIDANUS

Finding your way around the sky
You can start exploring around the sky when you have found just one well-known pattern of bright stars, such as Orion (the Hunter). Lines of bright stars, like those in Orion's belt, make helpful "signposts" to the constellations. Trace with your eyes the path from one bright star to another to discover more constellations. Soon you will learn to recognize lots of them.

BINOCULARS AND TELESCOPES

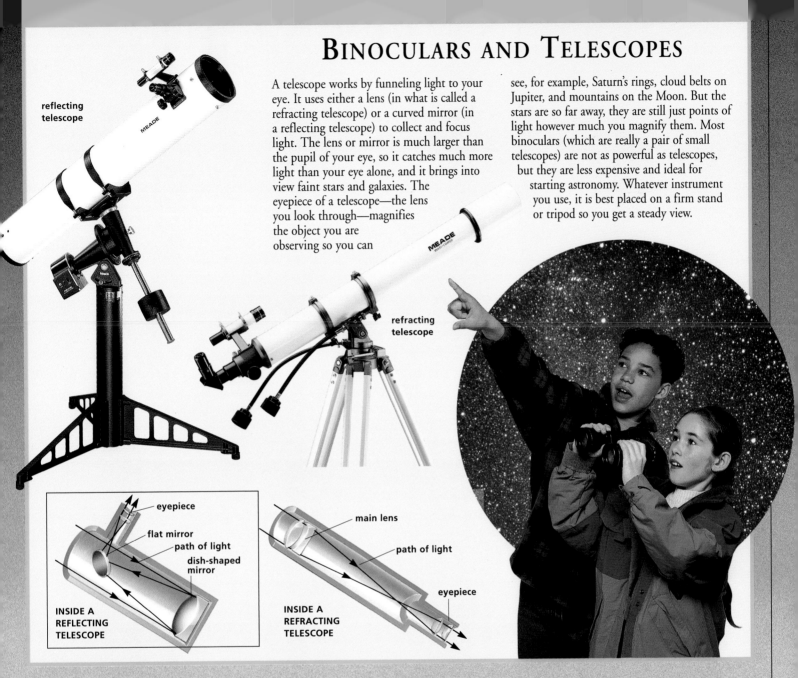

reflecting telescope

A telescope works by funneling light to your eye. It uses either a lens (in what is called a refracting telescope) or a curved mirror (in a reflecting telescope) to collect and focus light. The lens or mirror is much larger than the pupil of your eye, so it catches much more light than your eye alone, and it brings into view faint stars and galaxies. The eyepiece of a telescope—the lens you look through—magnifies the object you are observing so you can

see, for example, Saturn's rings, cloud belts on Jupiter, and mountains on the Moon. But the stars are so far away, they are still just points of light however much you magnify them. Most binoculars (which are really a pair of small telescopes) are not as powerful as telescopes, but they are less expensive and ideal for starting astronomy. Whatever instrument you use, it is best placed on a firm stand or tripod so you get a steady view.

refracting telescope

eyepiece
flat mirror
path of light
dish-shaped mirror

INSIDE A REFLECTING TELESCOPE

main lens
path of light
eyepiece

INSIDE A REFRACTING TELESCOPE

OBSERVING THE NIGHT SKY

On any clear night you can see fantastic sights. To find out which stars you can expect to see at a particular time, look at the star maps on pages 65–67. As you begin to observe the stars, you will notice that they twinkle. It happens because a star is a point of light, so its beam is easily disturbed by moving currents of air in our atmosphere. The best nights for observing with a telescope are when the air is fairly still so that the stars are not twinkling a lot.

Planets never seem to twinkle as much as stars. The planets are all much nearer to Earth than any star, so the beam of light reaching us from a

planet's disk is wider than the beam from a star and it flickers less. Their steady light helps you pick the planets out among the stars. Venus, Mars, Jupiter, and Saturn all get very bright in the sky from time to time and are good targets for a small telescope. Venus is regularly visible as a brilliant object in the east before dawn or in the west at dusk. Red Mars becomes bright for a few weeks roughly every other year: it takes a little over two years to track right around our sky, and for half the time it is too far away to be easily seen. Jupiter and Saturn change their positions slowly, and appear for several months every year.

If you are just starting to observe with binoculars, one of the best things to look at is the Moon. It is easy to pick out the largest craters and the dark seas. Try looking near the boundary between the bright and dark parts of the Moon (which is called the "terminator"). Here the mountains and craters look very dramatic. They cast long, dark shadows because the Sun's light is striking them at a low angle.

A few meteors can be seen most nights, but it is best to watch on a night when a meteor shower is due (see page 57). To observe meteors, you do not need a telescope at all—just warm clothes and a comfortable chair!

STARRY NIGHTS

Watch the stars for about an hour or more, and you will notice that the whole sky seems to be slowly wheeling over your head. The stars, like the Sun, rise in the east and set in the west. This nightly parade occurs because Earth spins. It takes just over 23 hours and 56 minutes for a star to return to the same position in our sky. For the Sun to do the same takes 24 hours because, as Earth spins, it also moves along its path around the Sun. This means that the stars rise four minutes earlier each day, and we see different stars as each night falls.

Around the north pole of the sky
This time-exposure photograph of the stars was taken over several hours with the camera pointing toward the north pole of the sky. As Earth turns, the stars appear to circle around the pole, so each one has made a trail like part of a circle. The smallest and brightest trail that can be seen in the photograph was made by the North Star, Polaris.

STARS THAT NEVER SET

Depending on where you are, some constellations stay above the horizon and never rise or set. Because they seem to circle constantly around the north or south pole of the sky, they are called circumpolar constellations. The Big Dipper in the constellation the Great Bear (or Ursa Major) is circumpolar for people in Canada and the northern U.S.A. From the southern U.S.A., the Big Dipper is partly below the horizon during late summer and fall. The Little Bear (Ursa Minor) is circumpolar from all places in North America and Europe.

STAR MAGNITUDES

To say how bright a star is, astronomers talk about its "magnitude." The brighter the star, the smaller is its magnitude—the brightest stars have magnitudes of –1 or less. The magnitude scale has been passed down from the Greek astronomer Hipparchus. In 120 B.C. he divided the stars into six groups according to their brightness. He did not have any instruments, so he judged as best he could by eye. Today, the scale has been made more precise. Stars with magnitudes over 6 are not visible with the naked eye.

THE NIGHT SKY AT DIFFERENT LATITUDES

What can you see?
There are stars all around us in every direction in space, but from Earth's surface we can see only half of them at a time. This is because the Earth itself blocks our view of the other half. Our view of the stars varies with our latitude (*see page 64*). Suppose

we start at a northern latitude, in New York or London, for example (**1**). Take a bright star about halfway between the point directly overhead and the horizon. If we then moved to the equator (**2**), the same star would appear above our heads.

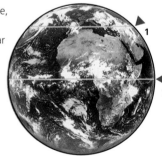

EARTH

BRIGHT STAR FACT FILE

THE BRIGHTEST STARS		
Name	**Constellation**	**Magnitude**
Sirius	Canis Major (the Great Dog)	–1.5
Canopus	Carina (the Keel)	–0.7
Alpha Centauri	Centaurus (the Centaur)	–0.3
Arcturus	Boötes (the Herdsman)	0.0
Vega	Lyra (the Lyre)	0.0
Capella	Auriga (the Charioteer)	0.1
Rigel	Orion (the Hunter)	0.1
Procyon	Canis Minor (the Little Dog)	0.4
Achernar	Eridanus (the River)	0.5
Betelgeuse	Orion (the Hunter)	0.5
Hadar	Centaurus (the Centaur)	0.6
Altair	Aquila (the Eagle)	0.8
Aldebaran	Taurus (the Bull)	0.9
Acrux	Crux (the Southern Cross)	0.9

1. an observer in the northern hemisphere

2. an observer near the equator

the same star is seen by both observers, but in a different part of the sky

SEASONAL STARS

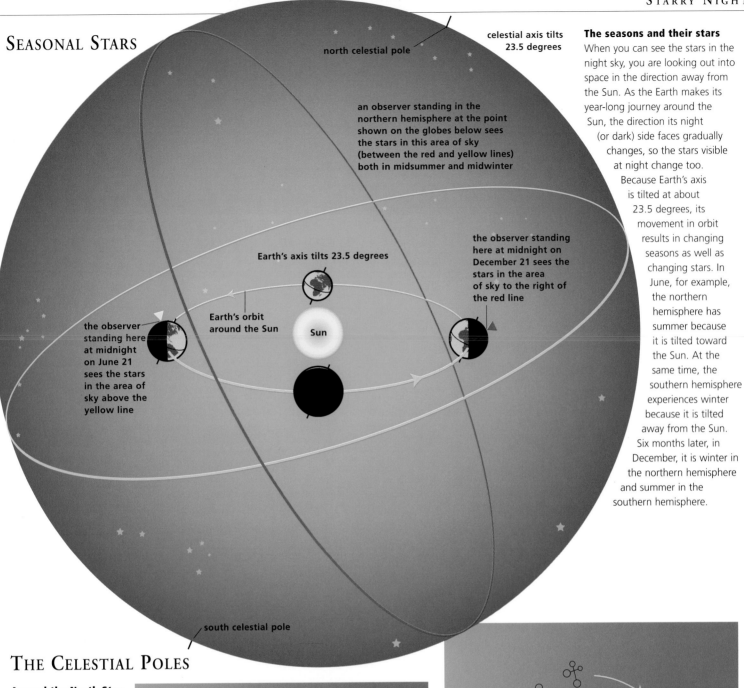

celestial axis tilts 23.5 degrees

north celestial pole

an observer standing in the northern hemisphere at the point shown on the globes below sees the stars in this area of sky (between the red and yellow lines) both in midsummer and midwinter

Earth's axis tilts 23.5 degrees

Earth's orbit around the Sun

Sun

the observer standing here at midnight on December 21 sees the stars in the area of sky to the right of the red line

the observer standing here at midnight on June 21 sees the stars in the area of sky above the yellow line

south celestial pole

The seasons and their stars

When you can see the stars in the night sky, you are looking out into space in the direction away from the Sun. As the Earth makes its year-long journey around the Sun, the direction its night (or dark) side faces gradually changes, so the stars visible at night change too. Because Earth's axis is tilted at about 23.5 degrees, its movement in orbit results in changing seasons as well as changing stars. In June, for example, the northern hemisphere has summer because it is tilted toward the Sun. At the same time, the southern hemisphere experiences winter because it is tilted away from the Sun. Six months later, in December, it is winter in the northern hemisphere and summer in the southern hemisphere.

THE CELESTIAL POLES

Around the North Star

The celestial poles are imaginary points in the sky directly above Earth's poles. From the northern hemisphere observers can see a bright star close to the north celestial pole. It is called Polaris, or the North Star. Because it is so close to the pole, Polaris hardly seems to move, while other stars circle around it over the course of a night. A famous pattern of stars near the north pole is the Big Dipper (or Plough), which is part of the Great Bear. Two of its stars point to Polaris.

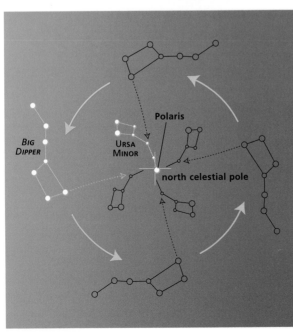

BIG DIPPER

URSA MINOR

Polaris

north celestial pole

CRUX

south celestial pole

Beta Centauri

Alpha Centauri

The Southern Cross

There is no bright star very near the south pole of the sky, but the famous constellation called Crux (the Southern Cross) is not far from the pole. One way to find the south celestial pole roughly is to imagine extending the long arm of the Southern Cross about five times its length.

PATTERNS OF STARS

Since earliest times, people in many lands have given their own names to the stars and have told stories about the patterns they make. Many names still used today were given by Greek and Arabic astronomers thousands of years ago. The Greek astronomer Ptolemy made a list of 48 constellations in the 2nd century A.D. They were mostly based on the myths of ancient Rome and Greece. Today astronomers use 88 constellations. Together they cover every part of the sky. The official names for these constellations are given in Latin, which was the language of the ancient Romans.

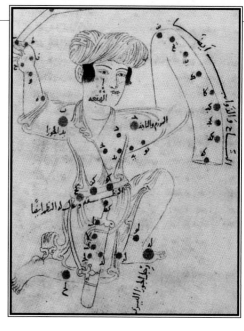

Ancient Arabic drawing of Orion
This thousand-year-old drawing of Orion (the Hunter) was made by the Arabic astronomer Al-Sufi. It shows Orion holding a curved sword. Al-Sufi wrote a list of 1,018 bright stars, and made illustrations like this one to show their positions.

STAR NAMES

Nearly all the brightest stars have their own names. Many come from names that were originally given by Arabic astronomers more than 1,000 years ago, such as Betelgeuse and Rigel in Orion. But bright stars also have names based on their constellations. In the 17th century, all the brightest stars were given a Greek letter (such as Alpha, Beta, or Gamma) followed by a form of their constellation name. So Betelgeuse is also known as Alpha Orionis, and Rigel as Beta Orionis. When astronomers ran out of Greek letters, they used numbers, so there are stars with names such as 32 Orionis and 60 Orionis. Today, there is no official way of giving a star an individual name. Faint stars just have numbers.

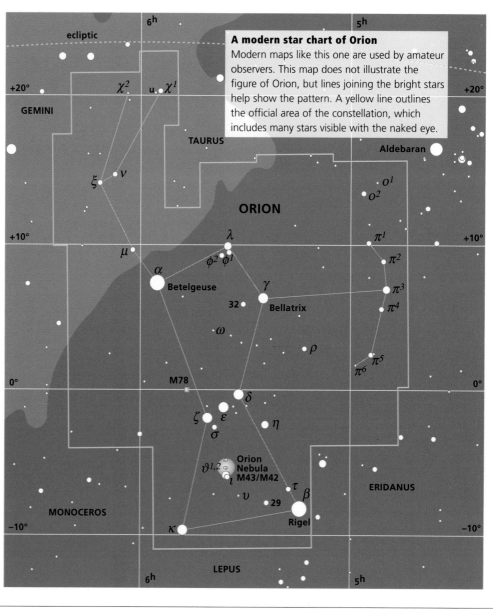

A modern star chart of Orion
Modern maps like this one are used by amateur observers. This map does not illustrate the figure of Orion, but lines joining the bright stars help show the pattern. A yellow line outlines the official area of the constellation, which includes many stars visible with the naked eye.

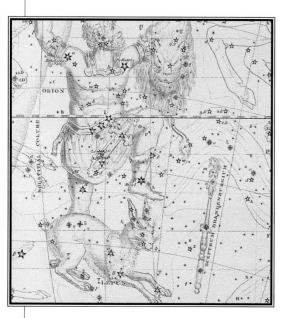

Orion in a 19th-century atlas
This picture of Orion is from a star atlas of 1822. In the middle, three bright stars make up Orion's belt, with the sword below. Several of the stars have the Arabic names given them by Al-Sufi (*see top right*). Below Orion lies the constellation Lepus (the Hare).

THE SUN'S PATH

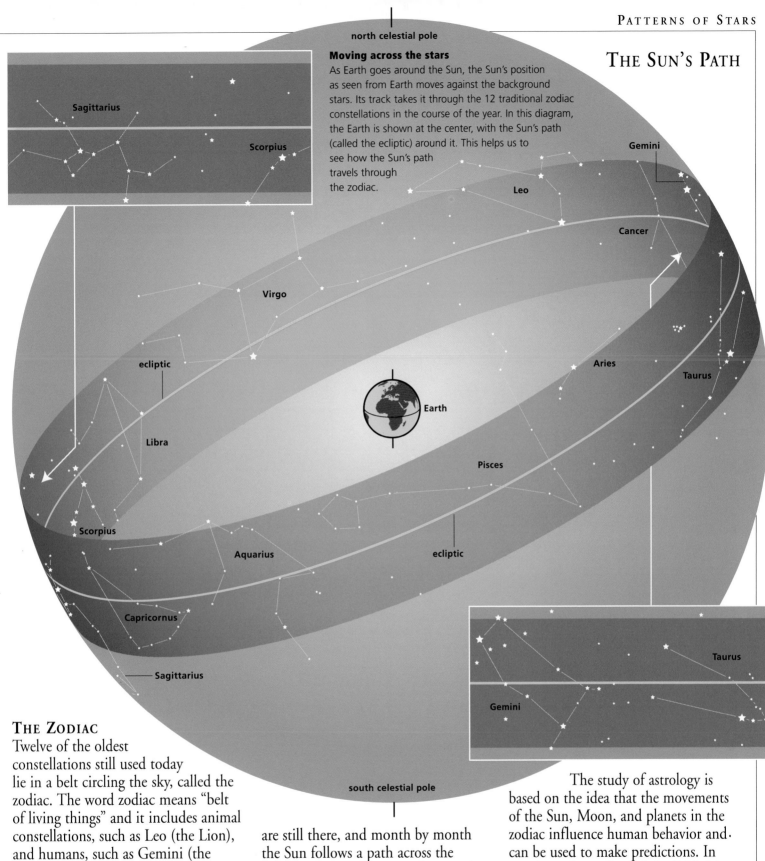

north celestial pole

Moving across the stars
As Earth goes around the Sun, the Sun's position as seen from Earth moves against the background stars. Its track takes it through the 12 traditional zodiac constellations in the course of the year. In this diagram, the Earth is shown at the center, with the Sun's path (called the ecliptic) around it. This helps us to see how the Sun's path travels through the zodiac.

Sagittarius

Scorpius

Gemini

Leo

Cancer

Virgo

Aries

Taurus

ecliptic

Libra

Earth

Pisces

ecliptic

Scorpius

Aquarius

Capricornus

Taurus

Sagittarius

Gemini

south celestial pole

THE ZODIAC
Twelve of the oldest constellations still used today lie in a belt circling the sky, called the zodiac. The word zodiac means "belt of living things" and it includes animal constellations, such as Leo (the Lion), and humans, such as Gemini (the Twins). The one non-living exception is Libra (the Scales).

Although some of the zodiac constellations contain only dim stars, their names are well known because they all lie on the Sun's yearly path around the sky. During the day, we cannot see the stars because the Sun's light drowns out starlight. But the stars are still there, and month by month the Sun follows a path across the 12 zodiac constellations. The Sun also goes through another constellation, Ophiuchus (the Serpent Bearer), which does not belong to the traditional zodiac. The Sun, Moon, and planets always lie somewhere along the zodiac or very close to it. Because of this, people long ago thought of it as a magical pathway through the stars.

The study of astrology is based on the idea that the movements of the Sun, Moon, and planets in the zodiac influence human behavior and can be used to make predictions. In astrology, the zodiac belt is divided into twelve equal sections called "signs." The signs have the same names as the twelve zodiac constellations, but they are no longer in the same positions since the Sun's path has shifted. There is no scientific evidence that the planets have any effect on us, and today, most people's interest in astrology is for fun.

STAR MAPS

These star maps are your guide to the brighter stars and the most well-known constellations. They will help you start skywatching. To keep the maps simple, they do not include all 88 constellations, just those that are easiest to find. You will be able to pick out many of them even if you are in a brightly lit town. The three sets of maps printed on the following pages show the stars you can see from different parts of the world during different seasons of the year.

Find your latitude band

To choose the right maps for you, you need to know which latitude band you are observing from. The most northerly band included in this book is 40°N to 60°N. Within this band lie New York, Chicago, Montreal, Vancouver, Madrid, London, and Paris. The middle band is 20°N to 40°N, and includes San Francisco, Los Angeles, Phoenix, and Dallas. The southern band, from 20°S to 40°S, includes most large cities in Australia and southern Africa.

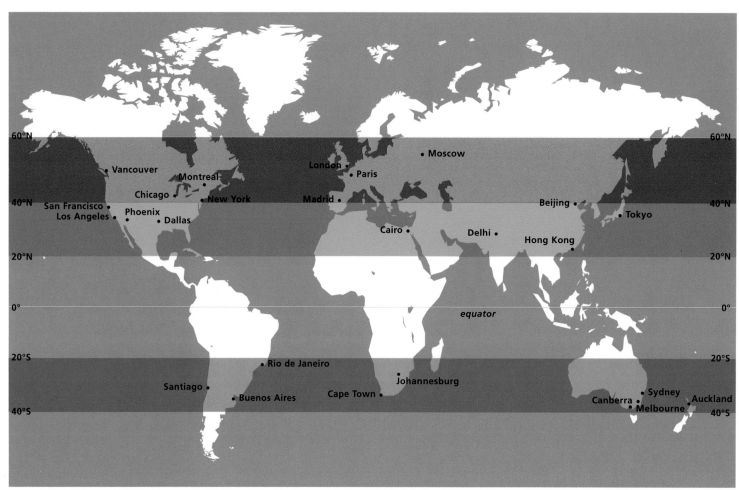

USING THE STAR MAPS

The stars you can see in a clear sky depend on three things: your latitude (which is the measure of how far north or south of the equator you are), the time of year, and the time of night. This book provides maps for three different latitude bands, so you first need to work out which band includes the latitude you are observing from. The world map above will help you do this. You will find the star maps for latitudes between 40°N and 60°N on

page 65, for 20–40°N on page 66, and for 20–40°S on page 67.

On the page of maps for your latitude, four pairs of semicircles show the constellations of the night sky for the four seasons. Choose the pair for the time of year when you are observing. The left-hand map shows the sky when you face north and the right-hand map gives the view of the sky toward the south. Notes next to the maps tell you the months and times of night when the maps are

exactly correct, but they are good enough to help you find the constellations at other times as well—just look for the maps with the nearest time and date. You will need to add one hour to the times shown here if you are on daylight saving time.

The size of the dots for the stars show their brightness—the larger the dot, the brighter the star. The Moon and the planets are not included on these maps because their positions change from year to year.

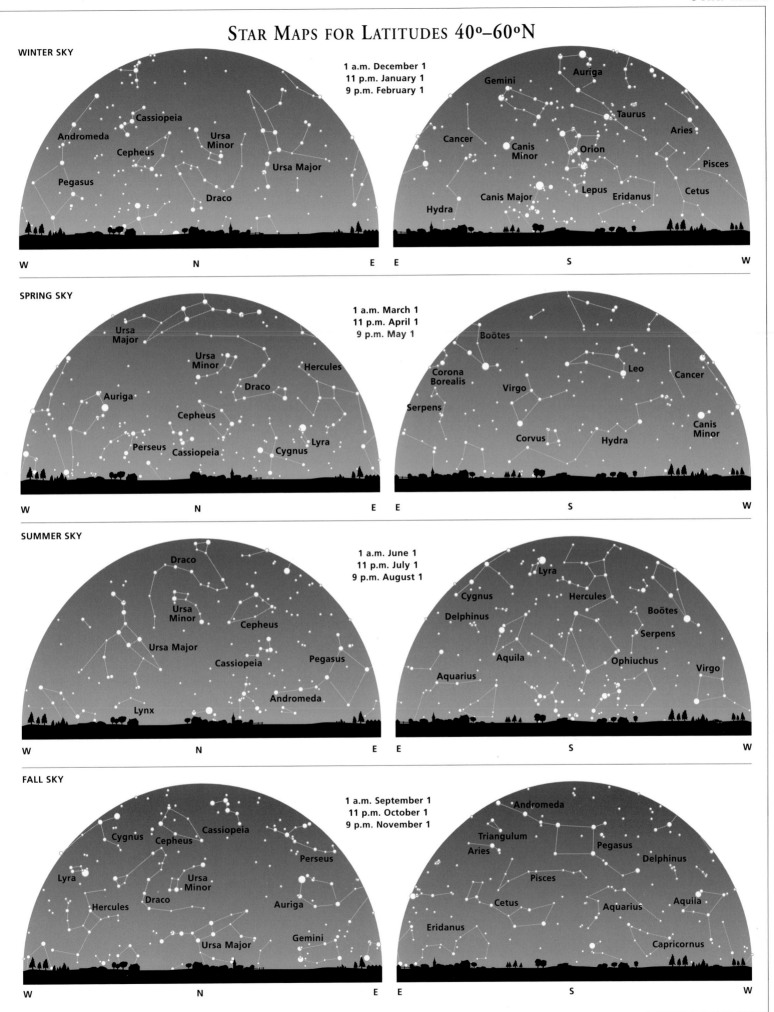

STAR MAPS FOR LATITUDES 40º–60ºN

WINTER SKY

1 a.m. December 1
11 p.m. January 1
9 p.m. February 1

SPRING SKY

1 a.m. March 1
11 p.m. April 1
9 p.m. May 1

SUMMER SKY

1 a.m. June 1
11 p.m. July 1
9 p.m. August 1

FALL SKY

1 a.m. September 1
11 p.m. October 1
9 p.m. November 1

STAR MAPS FOR LATITUDES 20°–40°N

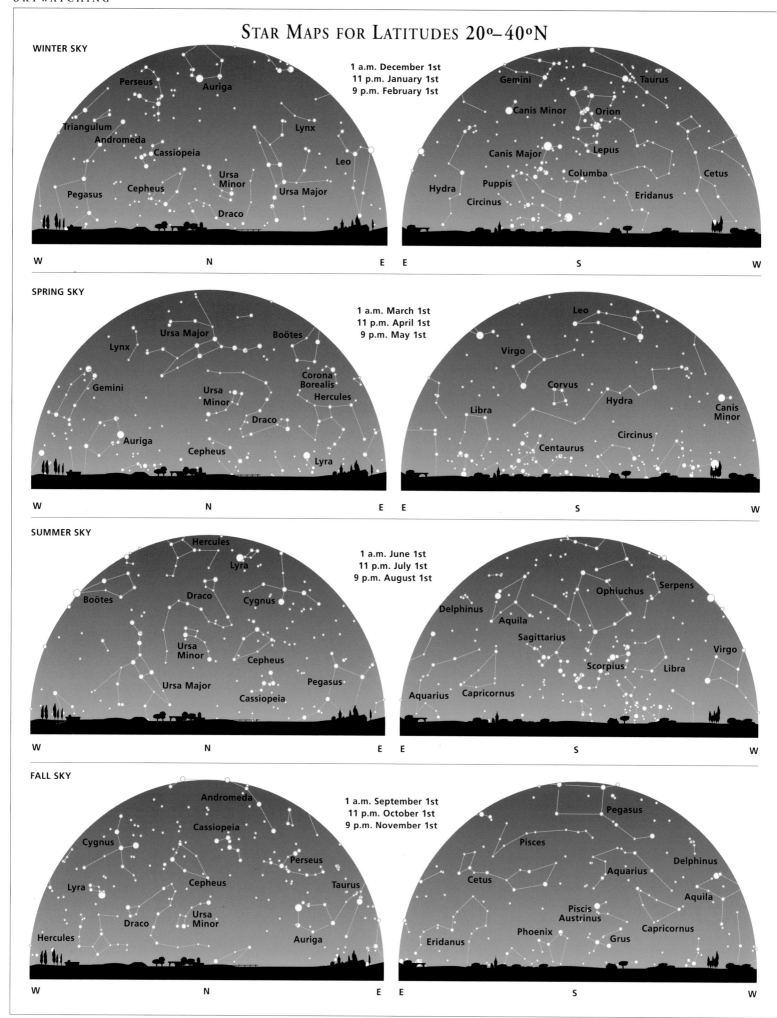

WINTER SKY

1 a.m. December 1st
11 p.m. January 1st
9 p.m. February 1st

Perseus · Auriga · Triangulum · Andromeda · Lynx · Cassiopeia · Leo · Ursa Minor · Ursa Major · Pegasus · Cepheus · Draco

W · N · E

Gemini · Taurus · Canis Minor · Orion · Canis Major · Lepus · Columba · Cetus · Hydra · Puppis · Circinus · Eridanus

E · S · W

SPRING SKY

1 a.m. March 1st
11 p.m. April 1st
9 p.m. May 1st

Ursa Major · Boötes · Lynx · Corona Borealis · Hercules · Gemini · Ursa Minor · Draco · Auriga · Cepheus · Lyra

W · N · E

Leo · Virgo · Corvus · Hydra · Libra · Canis Minor · Centaurus · Circinus

E · S · W

SUMMER SKY

1 a.m. June 1st
11 p.m. July 1st
9 p.m. August 1st

Hercules · Lyra · Boötes · Draco · Cygnus · Ursa Minor · Cepheus · Ursa Major · Cassiopeia · Pegasus

W · N · E

Ophiuchus · Serpens · Delphinus · Aquila · Sagittarius · Virgo · Scorpius · Libra · Aquarius · Capricornus

E · S · W

FALL SKY

1 a.m. September 1st
11 p.m. October 1st
9 p.m. November 1st

Andromeda · Cassiopeia · Cygnus · Perseus · Lyra · Cepheus · Taurus · Draco · Ursa Minor · Hercules · Auriga

W · N · E

Pegasus · Pisces · Aquarius · Delphinus · Cetus · Aquila · Piscis Austrinus · Capricornus · Eridanus · Phoenix · Grus

E · S · W

STAR MAPS FOR LATITUDES 20°–40°S

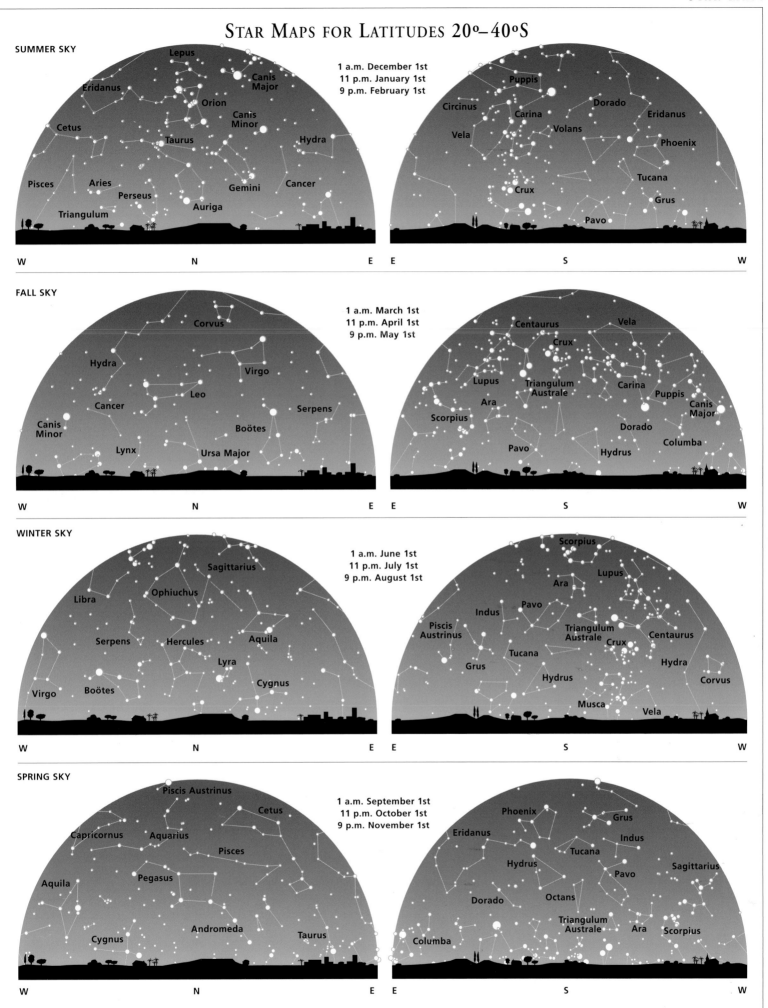

SUMMER SKY

1 a.m. December 1st
11 p.m. January 1st
9 p.m. February 1st

Lepus, Canis Major, Orion, Eridanus, Canis Minor, Cetus, Taurus, Hydra, Pisces, Aries, Perseus, Gemini, Cancer, Triangulum, Auriga

Puppis, Circinus, Carina, Dorado, Vela, Volans, Eridanus, Phoenix, Tucana, Crux, Grus, Pavo

W N E   E S W

FALL SKY

1 a.m. March 1st
11 p.m. April 1st
9 p.m. May 1st

Corvus, Hydra, Virgo, Cancer, Leo, Serpens, Canis Minor, Boötes, Lynx, Ursa Major

Centaurus, Vela, Crux, Lupus, Triangulum Australe, Carina, Puppis, Ara, Scorpius, Dorado, Canis Major, Pavo, Hydrus, Columba

W N E   E S W

WINTER SKY

1 a.m. June 1st
11 p.m. July 1st
9 p.m. August 1st

Sagittarius, Ophiuchus, Libra, Serpens, Hercules, Aquila, Virgo, Boötes, Lyra, Cygnus

Scorpius, Lupus, Ara, Pavo, Indus, Piscis Austrinus, Triangulum Australe, Centaurus, Crux, Tucana, Hydra, Grus, Corvus, Hydrus, Musca, Vela

W N E   E S W

SPRING SKY

1 a.m. September 1st
11 p.m. October 1st
9 p.m. November 1st

Piscis Austrinus, Cetus, Capricornus, Aquarius, Pisces, Aquila, Pegasus, Cygnus, Andromeda, Taurus

Phoenix, Grus, Eridanus, Indus, Tucana, Hydrus, Sagittarius, Pavo, Dorado, Octans, Triangulum Australe, Ara, Columba, Scorpius

W N E   E S W

PHASES AND ECLIPSES

The Moon takes four weeks to make one orbit of Earth. If you look at the Moon's position in the sky from night to night, you will see how it moves across different constellations. It completes a circle around the sky in 27 days, 7 hours, and 43 minutes. At the same time, the shape of the bright part of the Moon gradually changes from a thin crescent to a half Moon to a full Moon and back again. These are known as the phases of the Moon.

Sometimes you can see an eclipse of the Moon or the Sun. Though the Moon has to pass between Earth and the Sun every orbit, most times it does not lie in a completely straight line with them. When it is in line, the Moon hides all or part of the Sun's bright surface and we see a solar eclipse (an eclipse of the Sun). A lunar eclipse (an eclipse of the Moon) occurs when Earth lies between the Sun and a full Moon and casts its shadow on the Moon.

Sun

PHASES OF THE MOON

The Moon shines because it reflects sunlight. Only the half of the Moon that faces the Sun is lit up, and the amount we can see of it in our sky changes as the Moon orbits Earth. At new Moon you see none of it, but at full Moon you can see it all. Usually, the part of the Moon that is not being lit directly by the Sun is invisible, but sometimes it shines faintly when the Moon is a thin crescent. People call this "the old Moon in the young Moon's arms." The faint light is caused by "Earthshine," which is sunlight reflected by Earth. If you were on the Moon at this time, you would see a bright full Earth shining in your sky.

The time between two new Moons is 29 days, 12 hours, and 44 minutes, which is longer than the time it takes the Moon to circle the sky. This is because Earth travels about 45 million miles (72 million kilometers) along its orbit in a month, so that the Sun has moved on its path in the sky. The Moon needs just over two days to catch up to the Sun.

SOLAR AND LUNAR ECLIPSES

It's an amazing chance of nature that makes a total eclipse of the Sun occur. Though the Sun is 400 times larger than the Moon, it is also about 400 times farther away, so the Sun and Moon look roughly the same size from

△ **A total eclipse of the Moon**
Even when the Moon is in the darkest part of Earth's shadow during a total eclipse, it does not disappear from sight in the sky: it turns a dark orange or copper color. The Moon is reflecting a faint glow of sunlight scattered in its direction by Earth's atmosphere.

▷ **How eclipses work**
When the Moon comes directly between Earth and the Sun, its shadow falls on Earth, causing a solar eclipse. Where the main shadow (umbra) falls, there is a total eclipse. Places in the penumbra (partial shadow) see a partial eclipse. If the Moon passes through Earth's shadow when it is on the opposite side of Earth from the Sun, there is a lunar eclipse.

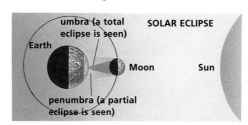

umbra (a total eclipse is seen)   **SOLAR ECLIPSE**
Earth
Moon   Sun
penumbra (a partial eclipse is seen)

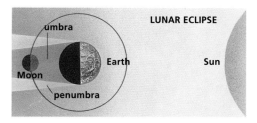

umbra   **LUNAR ECLIPSE**
Earth   Sun
Moon
penumbra

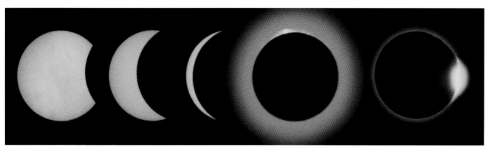

◁ **A total eclipse of the Sun**
From left to right, the first three photographs show the eclipse while it is still partial. The Moon gradually covers more of the Sun then moves directly in front of it. The eclipse is total and the sky is dark enough for the faint solar corona (see page 19) to be visible. The instant the total eclipse ends, a beam of sunlight bursts through a valley on the edge of the Moon. For a brief moment the effect is like a single sparkling diamond on a ring.

PHASES OF THE MOON

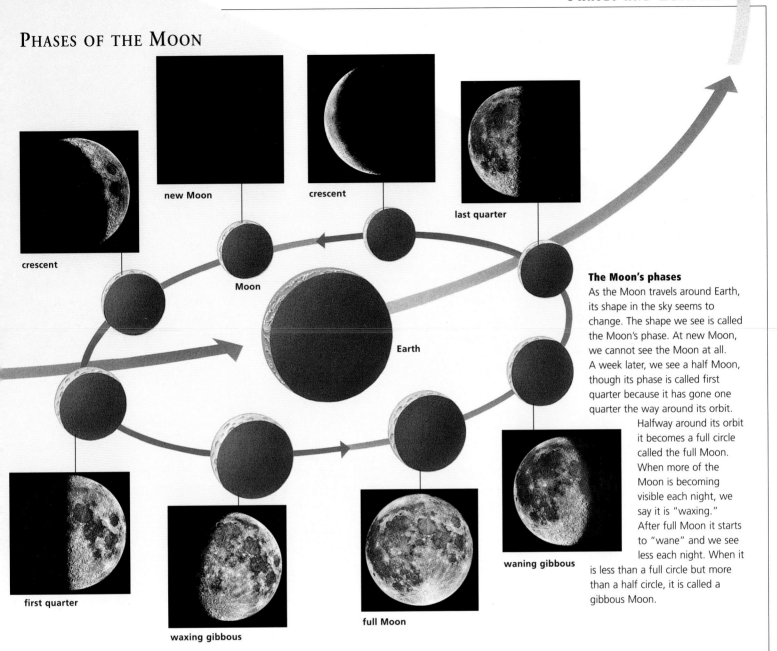

crescent

new Moon

crescent

last quarter

Moon

Earth

first quarter

waxing gibbous

full Moon

waning gibbous

The Moon's phases

As the Moon travels around Earth, its shape in the sky seems to change. The shape we see is called the Moon's phase. At new Moon, we cannot see the Moon at all. A week later, we see a half Moon, though its phase is called first quarter because it has gone one quarter the way around its orbit.

Halfway around its orbit it becomes a full circle called the full Moon. When more of the Moon is becoming visible each night, we say it is "waxing." After full Moon it starts to "wane" and we see less each night. When it is less than a full circle but more than a half circle, it is called a gibbous Moon.

Earth. A total solar eclipse reaches the point of "totality" when the Moon completely covers the visible disk of the Sun. With the sunlight blocked off, the sky goes dark and the faint light of the Sun's corona appears like a white halo around the dark circle of the Moon. Tongues of gas leaping out from the edge of the Sun may also be visible. Totality can last seven and a half minutes, though it is rarely this long.

There are always two solar eclipses in a year, sometimes more. Most of them are partial, when the Moon passes in front of the Sun but does not cover all of it for anyone watching anywhere on Earth. When solar eclipses are total, totality is only visible from a long, narrow area of Earth's surface, typically 100–200 miles (150–300 kilometers) wide though thousands of miles or kilometers long. Viewers over a much larger area see a partial solar eclipse.

Because the distances between Earth and the Sun and Moon vary a little, the Moon sometimes appears slightly smaller in the sky than the Sun. If this happens when the Moon crosses in front of the Sun, a ring of the Sun's disk stays visible and there is an annular eclipse (annular means ring shaped).

Up to seven eclipses can happen in a year. Two or three of them are lunar eclipses. An eclipse of the Moon can be total or partial, and it always looks the same from any place on Earth where the Moon happens to be up at the time of the eclipse.

DAY AND NIGHT

Sun

Spinning Earth

We have day and night because Earth turns as it orbits the Sun. In the diagram below, we are looking down on the north pole. Earth is traveling from left to right in its orbit around the Sun and turning counterclockwise at the same time. The four Earths are six hours apart. The dot shows how a place on the equator moves from midday, through night, to sunrise.

midday	sunset	midnight	sunrise

Earth

direction of the
Sun's light

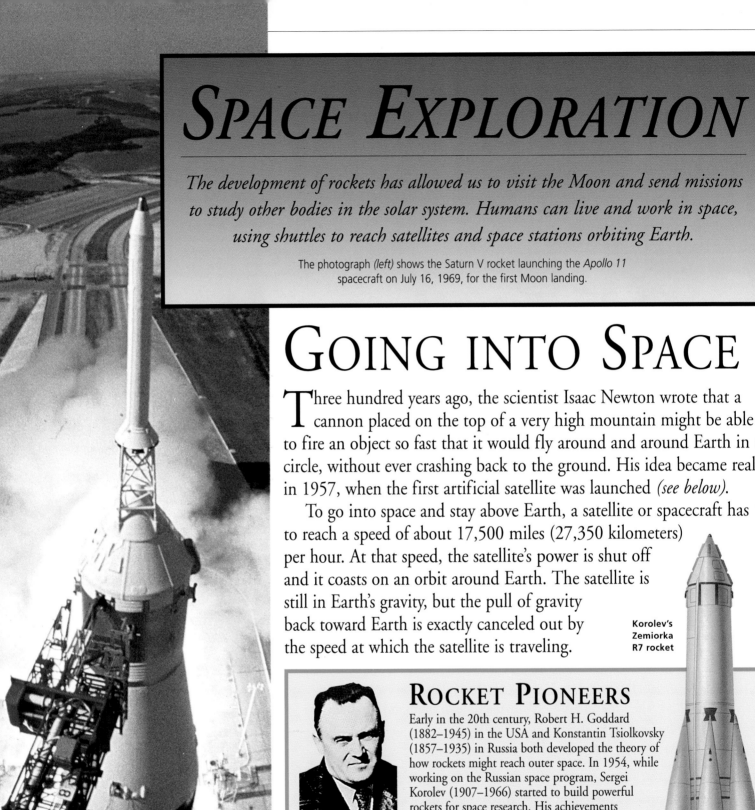

SPACE EXPLORATION

The development of rockets has allowed us to visit the Moon and send missions to study other bodies in the solar system. Humans can live and work in space, using shuttles to reach satellites and space stations orbiting Earth.

The photograph *(left)* shows the Saturn V rocket launching the *Apollo 11* spacecraft on July 16, 1969, for the first Moon landing.

GOING INTO SPACE

Three hundred years ago, the scientist Isaac Newton wrote that a cannon placed on the top of a very high mountain might be able to fire an object so fast that it would fly around and around Earth in a circle, without ever crashing back to the ground. His idea became reality in 1957, when the first artificial satellite was launched *(see below)*.

To go into space and stay above Earth, a satellite or spacecraft has to reach a speed of about 17,500 miles (27,350 kilometers) per hour. At that speed, the satellite's power is shut off and it coasts on an orbit around Earth. The satellite is still in Earth's gravity, but the pull of gravity back toward Earth is exactly canceled out by the speed at which the satellite is traveling.

Korolev's Zemiorka R7 rocket

ROCKET PIONEERS

Sergei Korolev

Wernher von Braun

Early in the 20th century, Robert H. Goddard (1882–1945) in the USA and Konstantin Tsiolkovsky (1857–1935) in Russia both developed the theory of how rockets might reach outer space. In 1954, while working on the Russian space program, Sergei Korolev (1907–1966) started to build powerful rockets for space research. His achievements include the first artificial satellite, *Sputnik-1*, in 1957, and the first landing on Venus, in 1966. Long-range rockets had been perfected in 1942 with the V2 built for the German Army by Wernher von Braun (1912–1977). At the end of World War II, von Braun and his team joined the Americans, and in 1955 they switched to space research. Von Braun was responsible for the first American satellites, the development of the mighty Saturn V launcher, and for directing the Apollo Moon missions.

von Braun's V2 rocket

SATELLITES IN ORBIT

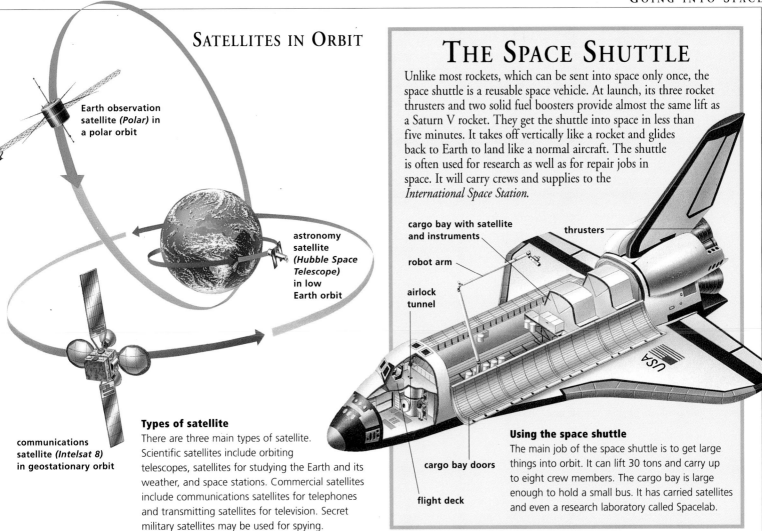

Earth observation satellite *(Polar)* in a polar orbit

astronomy satellite *(Hubble Space Telescope)* in low Earth orbit

communications satellite *(Intelsat 8)* in geostationary orbit

Types of satellite
There are three main types of satellite. Scientific satellites include orbiting telescopes, satellites for studying the Earth and its weather, and space stations. Commercial satellites include communications satellites for telephones and transmitting satellites for television. Secret military satellites may be used for spying.

THE SPACE SHUTTLE

Unlike most rockets, which can be sent into space only once, the space shuttle is a reusable space vehicle. At launch, its three rocket thrusters and two solid fuel boosters provide almost the same lift as a Saturn V rocket. They get the shuttle into space in less than five minutes. It takes off vertically like a rocket and glides back to Earth to land like a normal aircraft. The shuttle is often used for research as well as for repair jobs in space. It will carry crews and supplies to the *International Space Station.*

cargo bay with satellite and instruments

thrusters

robot arm

airlock tunnel

cargo bay doors

flight deck

Using the space shuttle
The main job of the space shuttle is to get large things into orbit. It can lift 30 tons and carry up to eight crew members. The cargo bay is large enough to hold a small bus. It has carried satellites and even a research laboratory called Spacelab.

LAUNCHING SATELLITES

Most artificial satellites are launched by rocket. A rocket carries the satellite to the right height above Earth, then sends it into orbit. The rocket then crashes back to Earth, usually landing in the ocean. The fastest planes can only get to one-tenth the speed needed to fly into space. A space rocket gets to a much higher speed by blasting out a huge amount of matter at very high speed for just a few minutes. The matter forced out through the rocket's engines thrusts the rocket forward so quickly that it can overcome Earth's gravity. Rocket engines are the only engines that can work in the airlessness of space.

Once in space, satellites are placed in different orbits to suit their job. A communications satellite may be placed in a high orbit above the equator, where it makes one orbit in exactly the same time it takes Earth to turn. As a result,

it stays in the same place above Earth. This is called a geostationary orbit. Satellites in polar orbits, circling Earth from pole to pole, can see all of Earth's surface as it spins. They are useful for studying weather systems and observing Earth's surface.

SPACE STATIONS

A space station is a complete environment for living and working, where astronauts can spend many months at a time in space. Inside, astronauts are weightless and must use exercise machines to keep their bones and muscles strong. The bathrooms are specially designed to work in the weightless environment, and the astronauts can wear everyday clothing. The U.S.A.'s first space station, *Skylab*, was placed in orbit in 1973. Over several years into the 21st century, sections of the *International Space Station* are being put together in space. The *International Space Station* is a joint project between the U.S. and 15 other nations.

Mir space station
Launched on February 20, 1986, the Russian space station *Mir* was made larger with new modules added over the years. It was badly damaged in a collision with a supply vehicle in 1997, but still managed to keep going until 1999.

MISSIONS IN SPACE

Spacecraft have visited the Sun, the Moon, planets, comets, and asteroids. They usually carry cameras and other instruments to gather information, which is beamed back to Earth by radio. Spacecraft are used in different ways. In a fly-by, a craft passes close to an object in space. An orbiter goes into orbit around a planet or Earth's moon and may work there for many years. Landers go down to the surface of a rocky planet or moon. A probe dropped into an atmosphere makes measurements as it falls.

EXPLORING THE SOLAR SYSTEM

MERCURY: *MARINER 10*

Mariner 10 is the only spacecraft that has gone to Mercury. It was the first mission to visit more than one planet. On the way to Mercury, *Mariner 10* photographed the clouds of Venus. It then went into an orbit of the Sun that allowed it to make three fly-bys of Mercury in 1974 and 1975. *Mariner 10* returned 2,700 photographs covering about a third of the surface of Mercury *(see page 33)*. It also detected the planet's magnetic field and measured its temperature.

THE SUN: *ULYSSES*

Launched by the space shuttle *Discovery* on October 6, 1990, this spacecraft was the first to explore the regions of space over the poles of the Sun. It could not be put straight into the correct orbit around the Sun, so *Ulysses* was first sent on a path that swept it past Jupiter. Jupiter's strong gravity boosted it into an orbit that passed over the Sun's south pole in 1994 and its north pole in 1995. *Ulysses* studies the solar wind *(see page 19)*.

VENUS: *PIONEER VENUS*

The *Pioneer Venus* mission explored the thick atmosphere of Venus. The spacecraft arrived on December 4, 1978. Its orbiter stayed above the clouds, using radar to map the surface of Venus and running several experiments to find out what the atmosphere is made of. The orbiter worked for almost 14 years before crashing into Venus. As well as the orbiter, there were four probes, which descended through the atmosphere measuring temperatures.

MISSIONS TO COMETS AND ASTEROIDS

The *Giotto* spacecraft was sent to Halley's Comet in 1986, and returned pictures until it got within about 400 miles (600 km) of the comet's nucleus *(see page 55)*. The *Near-Earth Asteroid Rendezvous (NEAR)* is the first spacecraft to orbit an asteroid, studying the asteroid Eros for one year from February 1999 *(see also pages 42–43)*. The Stardust mission of 1999 will collect some comet dust in space and bring it back to Earth.

NEAR

MARS: *VIKING 1* AND *VIKING 2*

One of the tasks of the Viking missions launched in 1975 was to search for life on Mars. Each spacecraft consisted of a lander and an orbiter. The orbiters' cameras mapped the planet in great detail. The landers tested the soil but found no clear evidence of life. They returned images for several years after landing.

THE MOON: *LUNAR PROSPECTOR*

Launched on January 5, 1998, *Lunar Prospector* was sent on a one-year mission to collect information about the composition of the Moon's surface and interior. The spacecraft was put in an orbit around the Moon at a height of 62 miles (100 km). Within a few weeks, one of its five instruments had found strong evidence that there are crystals of frozen water in rocks near the Moon's north and south poles.

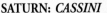

SATURN: *CASSINI*

Cassini was launched toward Saturn on October 15, 1997. It will arrive in July 2004. Then *Cassini* will swing close to the planet to begin the first of 60 orbits during its four-year mission. In late 2004, the spacecraft will drop a probe through the dense and cloudy atmosphere of Saturn's moon Titan *(see also page 49)*. *Cassini's* orbiter will make 30 close fly-bys of Titan and other moons of Saturn.

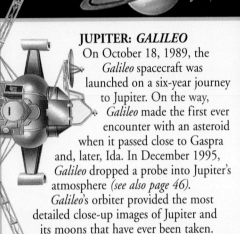

JUPITER: *GALILEO*

On October 18, 1989, the *Galileo* spacecraft was launched on a six-year journey to Jupiter. On the way, *Galileo* made the first ever encounter with an asteroid when it passed close to Gaspra and, later, Ida. In December 1995, *Galileo* dropped a probe into Jupiter's atmosphere *(see also page 46)*. *Galileo's* orbiter provided the most detailed close-up images of Jupiter and its moons that have ever been taken.

URANUS AND NEPTUNE: *VOYAGER 2*

Voyager 2, launched on August 20, 1977, made a tour of the four giant planets. It first flew past both Jupiter and Saturn before reaching Uranus on January 24, 1986, and Neptune on August 24, 1989. *Voyager 2* and its sister craft, *Voyager 1*, have continued to take measurements of the particles and magnetic fields in space as they speed farther from Earth. They are expected to send back data until 2020. *(See also page 45.)*

MORE MILESTONES IN THE EXPLORATION OF SPACE*

Sputnik-1, October 4, 1957
World's first artificial satellite. Launched by Russia.

Sputnik-2, November 3, 1957
Satellite takes first animal into orbit—a dog called Laika. Russia.

Explorer 1, February 1, 1958
First successful launch by U.S.

Luna 1, January 2, 1959
First fly-by of the Moon. Russia. Discovered the solar wind.

Luna 2, September 12, 1959
First spacecraft to hit the Moon. Russia.

Luna 3, October 4, 1959
Returned first pictures of the Moon's far side. Russia.

Venera 1, February 12, 1961
First fly-by of Venus. Russia.

Vostok 1, April 12, 1961
First human in space—Russian Yuri Gagarin.

Ranger 7, July 28, 1964
U.S. hard lander crash landed on the Moon. Sent back first detailed images of the Moon's surface as it approached.

Mariner 4, November 28, 1964
First fly-by of Mars—sent back 22 photographs showing cratered surface. U.S.

Venera 3, November 16, 1965
First object launched from Earth to reach another planet. Crash landed on Venus. Russia.

Luna 9, January 31, 1966
First soft lander (using parachutes or air bags to land gently) on the Moon. Sent back first photographs from the Moon's surface. Russia.

Surveyor 1, April 30, 1966
First U.S. soft lander on Moon.

Venera 4, June 12, 1967
First probe to return data on atmosphere and surface temperature of Venus. Russia.

Apollo 8, December 21, 1968
First humans go to the Moon and back, without landing on the Moon. U.S.

Apollo 11, July 16, 1969
First manned landing on Moon, followed by five more. U.S.

Venera 7, August 17, 1970
First successful landing on another planet (Venus). Russia.

Luna 16, September 12, 1970
First unmanned mission that returned sample of Moon dust to Earth. Russia.

Luna 17, November 10, 1970
First Moon landing with robotic explorer—Lunokhod 1. Russia.

Salyut 1, April 19, 1971
First space station. Russia.

Mariner 9, May 30, 1971
First spacecraft to orbit another planet—returned detailed images of Mars's surface. U.S.

Pioneer 10, March 3, 1972
First spacecraft to fly past Jupiter, returning 500 images. U.S.

Skylab, May 26, 1973
First U.S. space station, manned for 171 days.

Apollo 18 and Soyuz 19, July 15, 1975
First docking of U.S. and Russian spacecraft in orbit.

Viking 1, August 20, 1975
First successful lander on Mars. Returned images for six years. U.S.

Space shuttle Columbia, April 12, 1981
First successful use of a reusable space vehicle. U.S.

Mir space station, February 20, 1986
Launch of Russian space station—remained in continuous occupation until 1999.

Magellan, May 4, 1989
Carried out the first detailed mapping of the surface of another planet (Venus) by radar. Features only a quarter of a mile in size show up. U.S.

Hubble Space Telescope, April 25, 1990
Regularly returns detailed images of planets, moons, and comets. U.S./Europe.

Mars Pathfinder, December 4, 1996
First U.S. robotic exploration of the surface of another planet.

* Entries give dates of launches.

TELESCOPES AND OBSERVATORIES

Without telescopes we would know almost nothing about the universe. Light from distant objects in space is so faint by the time it reaches Earth that we need to collect it to build up a picture. An optical telescope collects light from an object and concentrates it, producing an enlarged image that can be seen by eye, photographed, or fed into a computer. Most objects in space send out much more than visible light, and special telescopes and detectors are used to pick up invisible radiation, such as radio waves, X rays, infrared radiation, and ultraviolet light.

Compton Gamma-Ray Observatory

In orbit
The *Compton Gamma-Ray Observatory (CGRO)*, launched by space shuttle in 1991, detects gamma rays, which are similar to X rays but are even more powerful. The *International Ultraviolet Explorer (IUE)* lasted longer than any other telescope put into space. Launched in 1978, it made ultraviolet observations for 18 years.

A NIGHT AT AN OBSERVATORY
A new telescope used by professional astronomers costs tens of millions of dollars, including its instruments and the dome that protects it. To get the clearest view, modern telescopes are located on high mountains where they are above as much of Earth's weather as possible, and far from large cities with their bright lights. Usually, several telescopes are grouped together at an observatory, which may be shared by several countries and many universities.

An astronomer will have spent several weeks planning a few nights of observing. As well as telescopes, an observatory has workshops and living quarters. Visiting astronomers may travel halfway around the world to get to one of the big telescopes at an observatory. The larger the main lens or mirror in a telescope, the greater the detail it can detect.

Professional astronomers working in observatories almost always capture the signal from a distant object

△ **Airborne observatories**
A high-flying plane is a good way of getting a telescope clear of most of the atmosphere. NASA's first airborne observatory flew between 1974 and 1996. A new one, called SOFIA *(pictured)*, will fly an infrared telescope 7 miles (12 km) high in a jumbo jet from the year 2001.

Canada-France-Hawaii Telescope

Clear skies at the Mauna Kea Observatory
Mauna Kea, on Hawaii, is at 13,800 feet (4,200 m) above sea level. First opened in 1970, this is one of the best places in the world for optical and infrared astronomy because the air is very dry and clear. The summit is home to eight large optical/infrared telescopes and two microwave telescopes. There is a radio telescope nearby.

Optical telescope
The Canada-France-Hawaii Telescope is one of the oldest on Mauna Kea. Opened in 1980, its mirror measures 141 inches (3.6 meters) across and it is shared by astronomers from Canada, France, and Hawaii.

Sub-millimeter (microwave) telescope
The James Clerk Maxwell Telescope is a gleaming reflector telescope measuring 49 feet (15 meters) across. It is the largest telescope in the world for observing sub-millimeter radio waves (a type of microwave). Microwaves are particularly important for understanding cool stars and gas clouds.

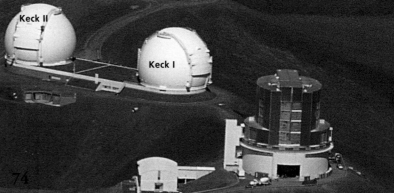

Keck II

Keck I

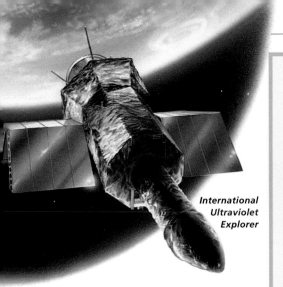

International Ultraviolet Explorer

ORBITING SPACE OBSERVATORIES

Astronomers working with invisible signals from space find that our atmosphere blocks out most infrared, ultraviolet, and X rays. Astronomers working with visible light have to put up with unsteady images, because the atmosphere makes the stars twinkle. One answer to these problems is to put telescopes above the atmosphere, on an orbiting satellite or space observatory. Space observatories are expensive, mainly because of the high costs of launching them. There also has to be a network of communications dishes spread out at different locations around the world to control them as they orbit Earth once every 90 minutes.

Some important space observatories:

Einstein Observatory (X rays) 1978–1981
IUE (International Ultraviolet Explorer) 1978–1996
IRAS (Infrared Astronomical Satellite) 1983
COBE (Cosmic Background Explorer) 1989–
Hipparcos (star positions and movements) 1989–1993
ROSAT (Roentgen Satellite—X rays) 1990–
CGRO (Compton Gamma-Ray Observatory) 1991–
HST (Hubble Space Telescope) 1992–
ISO (Infrared Space Observatory) 1995–1998
SOHO (Solar and Heliospheric Observatory) 1995–
RXTE (Rossi X ray Timing Explorer) 1995–
Beppo-SAX (X rays) 1996–
AXAF (Advanced X ray Astronomy Facility) 1998–

electronically. This means that the information obtained is immediately entered into a computer system to be analyzed later. Electronic detectors are better than photography or the naked eye at collecting light that is very faint.

All telescopes need something to collect the signals. Radio telescopes normally have large dishes. The dish concentrates the signals and feeds them into a special radio receiver. With the help of a computer, the signals can be turned into a picture showing, for example, how a galaxy would appear if we could see its radio waves.

If all goes well, several dozen stars or galaxies will be observed in one night. The results from one night of observing will provide months of work for the astronomer, who will often compare the data with information from other kinds of telescope.

Major observatory sites on Earth

The major astronomical observatories with optical and infrared telescopes (red dots) are on high mountains or extinct volcanoes where the air is clearest. Important sites include the Canary Islands, Hawaii, Chile, and southern Arizona. It does not matter so much where radio telescopes (blue dots) are built, since radio waves can pass through clouds. Several radio telescopes at different places around the world can be linked together to look at an object in far greater detail than is possible with one telescope.

Jodrell Bank, England
Zelenchukskaya, Russia
Kitt Peak, Mt. Graham, Mt. Hopkins, Arizona
Calar Alto, Spain
Palomar Mountain, California
Green Bank, West Virginia
La Palma, Canary Islands
Very Large Array, New Mexico
Mauna Kea, Hawaii
Arecibo, Puerto Rico
Cerro Paranal and La Silla, Chile
Cerro Tololo, Chile
Siding Spring, Australia
Parkes, Australia

LOCATIONS OF IMPORTANT OBSERVATORIES

ON THE GROUND

Some important ground-based telescopes:

Keck I and Keck II, Mauna Kea, Hawaii *(see page 5)*.

Bolshoi Teleskop Azimutalnyi, Zelenchukskaya, Russia. Largest single-mirror reflecting telescope. Mirror 20 feet (6 m) across. Opened: 1975.

Hale Telescope, Palomar Mountain, California. Mirror 200 inches (5 m) across. Opened in 1948, was largest optical telescope in the world for 28 years.

Yerkes Telescope, Wisconsin. Largest telescope with a lens (refractor) ever built (1897). Lens 40 inches (1 m) across.

The Very Large Telescope, Cerro Paranal, Chile. Set of four telescopes each with 27-foot (8.2-m) mirrors, but linked together so equal to a single telescope with a 54-foot (16.4-m) reflector. Completion: 2001.

Green Bank Telescope, Green Bank, W. Virginia. Largest fully steerable radio dish; 325 feet (100 m) across. Completion: 1998.

Arecibo Telescope, Puerto Rico. Largest radio astronomy dish in the world, built into natural hollow in the ground. Dish 1,000 feet (305 m) across. Completion: 1963.

Very Large Array, near Socorro, New Mexico. Largest array of radio telescopes (27 dishes) on one site. Opened: 1981. *(See also page 14.)*

James Clerk Maxwell Telescope, Mauna Kea, Hawaii *(see page 74)*.

Radio telescope
The Very Long Baseline Array is a network of ten radio telescopes stretching from north-eastern Canada to Hawaii, all controlled remotely from Socorro, New Mexico. Each station has an 82-foot (25-meter) diameter dish (which radio astronomers call an antenna). The ten dishes work together as the world's largest astronomical instrument. It can pinpoint objects sending out radio waves with enormous accuracy.

GLOSSARY

asteroid A rocky object orbiting the Sun. Asteroids are similar to planets but much smaller. They are also called minor planets.

astronaut A person who travels into space. A Russian astronaut is called a cosmonaut.

astronomer A person who studies astronomy.

astronomy The study of the universe and all the things in it beyond Earth.

atmosphere A layer of gas around the outside of a planet or star.

average A middle value of a range from the highest to the lowest values. For example, Earth's average temperature is a middle value between its coldest and hottest temperatures.

axis The imaginary line around which a spinning object (such as a planet) rotates.

billion One thousand million.

black hole A tiny volume of space into which a huge amount of material is packed. Its gravity is so strong that nothing escapes from it—not even light. Astronomers have found two kinds of black hole: star-sized black holes, which contain several times the mass of the Sun, and supermassive black holes in the centers of galaxies, which have as much material as thousands or millions of Suns.

celestial To do with the sky.

cluster A family of stars or galaxies, held together in space because the gravity of each member of the cluster pulls on all the others.

comet A frozen chunk of ice and dust that orbits the Sun and releases a cloud of gas and dust when it travels near enough to the Sun to be warmed by the Sun's heat. The gas and dust streams out into space to form tails.

constellation One of 88 recognized star patterns that together cover every part of the sky.

core A region in the very middle of something. It is often of a different material from the material that surrounds it.

crater A bowl-shaped hollow on the surface of a planet or moon. Craters are formed when rocks from space crash onto a planet or when material collapses down inside the top part of a volcano.

crust The thin outside layer of something.

diameter The largest distance from one side to the other of a circle or sphere.

elements (chemical) The basic materials that make up all matter in the universe. Hydrogen, carbon, and oxygen are examples of elements. Chemical elements combine together to form other materials. For example, carbon dioxide is formed from carbon and oxygen.

ellipse A shape that looks like a squashed circle. Ellipses range in shape from extremely long and thin to very nearly circular.

elliptical Having the shape of an ellipse.

energy What it takes to make something move or to heat something up.

equator An imaginary line that circles a planet halfway between its north and south poles.

galaxy A family of billions of stars on its own in space. Some galaxies also have large quantities of gas and dust between the stars.

gas (see matter)

gravity A pulling force that acts between all objects in the universe. The force of gravity between two things gets stronger the closer they are together and the greater the amount of material they contain.

greenhouse effect The effect created in the atmosphere of a planet by some gases that trap the Sun's heat and warm up the planet. Some gases, such as carbon dioxide, create an especially strong greenhouse effect.

hemisphere Half of a sphere. On a planet, the northern hemisphere lies to the north of the equator and the southern hemisphere lies to the south.

infrared light A type of light that is invisible to human eyes. All warm things give out infrared rays and we feel them as warmth on our skin.

interstellar material Gas and dust between the stars.

latitude A measurement that shows how far north or south of the equator a place is. It is measured in degrees. The latitude of the equator is 0 degrees and the latitude of the north pole is 90 degrees north.

lava Liquid rock that flows out of a volcano. Lava is liquid because it is very hot when it comes up from inside Earth. It turns to solid rock when it cools down at Earth's surface.

lens A piece of shaped glass, or other transparent material, used to collect light and direct it in a particular way. Binoculars and refracting telescopes use lenses to collect light and bring it to a focus.

light A form of energy that can travel on its own even through empty space. Humans can see visible light, but there are forms of light that human eyes cannot see. These include infrared and ultraviolet light.

light year The distance light travels in one year. Light moves at just over 186,000 miles (about 300,000 km) per second and travels about 5.9 million million miles (9.5 million million km) in a year.

liquid (see matter)

lunar On the Moon or to do with the Moon.

magnetic field A region where magnetism acts.

magnetism A force that acts around magnetized materials (such as a solid piece of iron) and around materials in which electric currents are flowing (such as a wire or the metal core inside a planet). Magnetic forces can be attractive (pulling toward) or repulsive (pushing away).

mantle The main layer of rock that lies under the crust of a planet and above the core.

mass The amount of material in something.

matter All material. Matter makes up all things in the universe, whether gas, liquid, or solid. A **gas** can flow and move very easily. It will expand to fill a larger space. The air we breathe is a gas made up of a mixture of different chemicals. A **liquid** can flow easily, but unlike a gas, it does not expand if moved to a larger space. A **solid** cannot flow, and keeps its shape. Nearly all materials can change between being a gas, a liquid, or a solid according to their temperature and pressure. On Earth, for example, we have water as a solid (ice), liquid, or gas (water vapor).

meteor A bright streak visible for a few seconds in the night sky. It is caused by a piece of space dust or rock speeding into Earth's atmosphere, where it burns up.

meteorite A chunk of rock from space that lands on the surface of a planet or moon.

meteoroid A small piece of rock in space.

microscopic Describing something that is so small you need a microscope to see it.

Milky Way A faint hazy band across the night sky where we see the light of huge numbers of stars in the galaxy to which our Sun belongs. We call our galaxy the Milky Way Galaxy.

molten In the form of a liquid. It is used particularly to describe something that is normally solid, but has become a liquid because it has been heated.

moon A natural body orbiting a planet. Moons are also called natural satellites. The Moon (with a capital "M") is Earth's natural satellite.

naked eye Observing with just the eyes and without the help of a telescope or binoculars.

nebula (plural **nebulae**, pronounced neb-you-lee) A cloud of gas or dust in space. *Nebula* is the Latin word for cloud. Bright nebulae are glowing gas. Dark nebulae are clouds of fine dust.

nuclear energy Energy that can be released from the tiny particles that make up all matter. The Sun and stars make nuclear energy in their centers, where it is very hot and particles of hydrogen gas crash together.

nucleus Something at the very center of an object—it is small and concentrated compared with the rest of the object.

observatory A place where astronomers use telescopes or have their offices.

optical To do with light that we can see.

orbit The path taken by one object around another in space, because the two are attracted together by the pull of gravity.

particle A very small piece of matter.

planet A body that orbits the Sun or another star, and does not give out any of its own light.

pole The poles of a planet or moon are the places where the axis on which it spins meets the surface. There is a north pole and a south pole. The celestial poles are the points in the sky directly above the north and south poles of the planet's or moon's surface.

pressure The strength of the force with which something presses. A gas presses on anything in it and on its container (if it is in one). The pressure of a gas becomes higher when it is squashed into a smaller space, and when it is heated to a higher temperature.

radiation Beams of energy, such as visible light or X rays.

radio waves A form of energy that travels on its own through space and is invisible.

satellite A small object that orbits something larger. Artificial satellites are human-made objects put into orbit around Earth. Astronomers call the moons that travel around planets "natural satellites." There are small galaxies that are the satellites of much larger galaxies.

solar To do with the Sun.

solar system The Sun and everything that orbits around it. The solar system includes the nine major planets and their moons, asteroids, comets, meteoroids, and dust—all held in their orbits by the pull of the Sun's gravity.

solid *(see matter)*

space Everywhere beyond Earth's atmosphere.

star A large ball of hot gas that gives off light and heat because it is generating nuclear energy deep inside. A ball of gas has to contain at least one twentieth the amount of material in the Sun to become a star.

stellar To do with the stars.

supernova (plural **supernovae**, pronounced super-no-vee) A massive star that has exploded. A single supernova can give out as much light as billions of ordinary shining stars.

ultraviolet light A type of light that is given off by very hot objects and is invisible to human eyes. Ultraviolet light is more powerful than visible light and harms living things. The Sun gives out ultraviolet light. Most of it is stopped by Earth's atmosphere, though some of it gets through. Ultraviolet light causes sunburn.

universe All of space and everything in it, including Earth.

volume The amount of space that something takes up.

X rays A form of energy that travels on its own through space. X rays are similar to light but are invisible and are very much more powerful.

INDEX

ACKNOWLEDGMENTS

ILLUSTRATIONS

Richard Chasemoore, 33, 35 (top left and top center), 44 (bottom left), 45 (box image), 54, 56, 58–59 (background), 74 (center); **Chris Forsey,** 48 (center); **Gary Hincks,** 32 (bottom), 35 (bottom); **Rob Jakeway,** cover, 7, 8–9 (background image), 13 (box images), 15 (main image), 16–17, 18–19, 21, 26 (box image), 27 (top), 30–31, 38–39 (bottom), 42 (top right), 46, 48–49, 53 (top), 74–75 (top); **Peter Sarson,** 50; **Guy Smith,** 9 (bottom right), 10–11, 22–23, 28 (bottom left), 32 (center), 35 (top right), 44 (center), 52 (center), 55 (bottom), 59 (box images), 68–69, 70–71, 72–73; **Roger Stewart,** 5 (bottom right), 12 (box images), 15 (inset and box images), 24–25, 26, 27 (bottom), 28–29, 39 (top), 43, 53 (bottom); **Wil Tirion,** 60–61, 62–63, 64–65, 66–67.

PHOTOGRAPHS

1 = left; r = right; b = bottom; t = top; c = center

1(title page) NASA; 2t Digital Vision; 2b Bruce Balick University of Washington/NASA; 4l ROE/AAT; 4c & 4r Digital Vision; 4/5c Lund Observatory; 5tl Roger Ressmeyer/Corbis; 5tr & cl Digital Vision; 5cr Corbis-Bettmann; 5bl NASA; 5bc David Malin/Royal Observatory Edinburgh; 5br D.A.Calvert, Royal Greenwich Obseryatory/Science Photo Library; 6t NASA; 6c, bc, & r Digital Vision; 6b Tony Stone Images; 7t & 7r NASA; 7l Digital Vision; 9t Department of Astrophysics,University of Oxford; 9b Digital Vision; 10 AAO/ROE; Photo from UK Schmidt, plates by David Malin; 11c Science Photo Library; 11r Tony & Daphne Hallas/Science Photo Library; 11b David Malin/Royal Observatory Edinburgh, Anglo Australian Telescope; 12c David Malin/Anglo Australian Observatory; 12r Anglo Australian Observatory, photograph by David Malin; 13t NASA; 13tl European Southern Observatory; 13cl Anglo Australian Telescope Board; 13b Digital Vision; 13bl David Malin/Anglo Australian Observatory; 13c David Malin Anglo Australian Observatory; 14tl Buddy Mays/Corbis; 14tr NRAO/AUI/J.O.Burns/E.J.Shreier/E.D.Feigelson; 14b NASA; 16/17t Anglo Australian Telescope Board; 17cr & b NASA; 18 NASA; 19t The SOHO-ETT Consortium: SOHO is an ESA/NASA project of International Co-operation; 19c NASA; 19b ZEFA; 20t David Malin/Royal Observatory Edinburgh; 20c Roger Ressmeyer/Corbis; 20b Digital Vision; 20/21 Digital Vision; 21 NASA; 24 Space Telescope Science Institute/NASA/Science Photo Library; 25l NASA; 25c AAO/ROE, Photo from UK Schmidt, plates by David Malin; 25r Harvard University Library; 28tr Digital Vision; 28tl Jonathan Blair/Corbis; 28b Smithsonian Institution/Science Photo Library; 29t NASA; 29c NOAO/N.A.Sharp/G.Jacoby; 29b Californian Institute of Technology & Carnegie Institution of Washington; 30l NASA/JPL/Malin Space Science Systems; 32 & 33 NASA; 34t Digital Vision; 34b David P.Anderson, SMU/NASA/Science Photo Library; 35 Digital Vision; 36l UPI/Corbis; 36r Tony Stone Images/Richard Kaylin; 36b NASA; 36/37 background Tony Stone Images/Bob Barbour; 37tr Tony Stone Images; 37c ZEFA-Stockmarket; 38 Digital Vision; 39 NASA; 40l & b NASA; 40r Digital Vision; 41tl UPI/Corbis-Bettmann; 41tr Royal Astronomical Society Library; 41l & c NASA; 41cl NASA/Science Photo Library; 41cr NASA/Science Photo Library; 42l & c NASA/JPL; 42r NASA; 43r NASA; 45t & b NASA; 45c Digital Vision; 46 NASA; 47bl & c Digital Vision; 47cr & br NASA; 49 NASA; 50l National Maritime Museum Picture Library; 50r NASA; 51 NASA; 54 Pekka Parviainen/Science Photo Library; 55t NASA; 55bl E.T.Archive; 55br European space Agency/Science Photo Library; 56t The Natural History Museum, London; 56b NOAO/Science Photo Library; 57tl & b The Natural History Museum, London; 57tr Francois Gohier/Science Photo Library; 57c NASA/Science Photo Library; 58 & 59tr Frank Zullo/Science Photo Library; 59tc Meade Instruments; 60l Richard Cummins/Corbis; 60r NASA; 62t Bodleian Library; 62l Mary Evans Picture Library; 68l Roger Ressmeyer/Corbis; 68r John Sanford/Science Photo Library; 69 Lick Observatory, University of California; 70l NASA; 70tc Science Photo Library; 70bc NASA/Science Photo Library; 71 NASA/Science Photo Library; 74/75 background & 74l John Sanford/Science Photo Library; 74r Royal Observatory, Edinburgh; 75 Roger Ressmeyer/Corbis.